Nuts & Bolts of Rodent Control & Bugs & Other Stuff: Volume II

by

Lyle L. Townsend

"U DO IT"

YOURSELF PEST CONTROL MANUAL

(SAVE MONEY AND DO IT RIGHT)

DORRANCE
PUBLISHING CO
EST. 1920
PITTSBURGH, PENNSYLVANIA 15238

Dorrance Publishing Co
585 Alpha Drive
Suite 103
Pittsburgh, PA 15238
Visit our website at *www.dorrancebookstore.com*

ISBN: 978-1-6386-7330-9
eISBN: 978-1-6386-7358-3

TABLE OF CONTENTS

ABOUT THE AUTHOR

Lyle Townsend has been in the pest control business since 1967. He purchased his company from his uncle shortly after high school. Lyle has a masters license issued by King County Washington State Health Department, he is the thirty-eighth licensee in the history of Seattle, Washington, and a Washington State trappers license. He held a State of Washington Applicators license until 2005, after transferring his operation to Las Vegas, Nevada, and he obtained a state Principal license and is still active in pest control to present. He has been lecturing on pest control around the country for various suppliers and state associations from as early as 1971. During the '90s, Lyle invented several different tools for pest controllers such as a bait station that he calls the "Rodent Rock". The station simulates a landscape rock that is used as a rodent bait station and can be used outside to blend into the landscape without changing the aesthetics. He also invented a special mole trap that is accepted in most states for its ability to eliminate moles without being a hazard to the user. It's called the Annie Missile mole trap. He holds several patents on pest control equipment he has invented over the years.

During Lyle's career he has studied IPM and made many advances on its use in pest control that have made procedures quick and easy to eliminate rodents and other pests with the use of less toxicants.

DEDICATION

Dedicated to my father who is now passed away. He was in the pest control business for thirty-seven years, and while I was a teenager he made a lasting impression on me on always trying to help his fellow man. He was always willing to go out of his way to show his competitors alike his methods.

THE BEGINNINGS

When I was a young boy of sixteen years old, my father had been in the pest control industry for about ten years at that time, and on Saturdays sometimes he would let me ride along with him on his pest control route. On days that he would do rodent work I would tag along and help him carry his box of bait, and on occasion he would have me pick up and refresh the bait in the boxes that were used back then. Most of them were home made of wood, and some were made of prefabricated cardboard that he would buy from his suppliers. This was a few years before EPA existed, and before there was any real government standards that the pest control companies had to follow. Back then everyone essentially made up the procedures as they went. Speaking from the experience I have had over the years, I would say we have come a long way in truly protecting our environment, and reducing unnecessary risks that our forefathers dealt with. As I got into my twenties, I became very active in pest control with my uncle who also owned a company. Shortly after I went to work for him, he passed away, and I purchased the business from his estate. That was in 1967. One of the problems that always bothered me was many of the companies baited in attics, and crawlspaces, and inside the garages, and even inside the kitchen. I know a lot of the time one can get lucky and nothing becomes of this practice, but sometimes it can backfire and a rat will die under a kitchen cabinet, or in a wall or in the ceiling between floors. This can lead to a horrible smell and an unhappy customer. In the '70s I happened to pick up a state pest control manual and it explained IPM (Integrated Pest Management). Its approach was very simple... It described how you could change the environment so the rats will not be interested in the area for harborage. Closing off openings made total sense to me, so I began to approach the problem in that fashion.

TREATING INSIDE:

As a general rule, make sure that you understand what is being done, and if vacating the premises is necessary that all people and pets are out of the house before you start spraying and until the surfaces are completely dry, and ventilated when odor products are used. Always ask if anyone has upper respiratory illnesses, or the chemical product requires the premises be vacated during the treatment, and the occupants must not return until the product has dried, and the rooms well ventilated. People with upper respiratory illness may need to be out longer than one day.

** Fish tanks or bowls should be covered with a newspaper, sheet or towel and the air pump turned off. The air intake for the tank should be raised above the floor to avoid spraying it.

** Birds are very susceptible to pesticides so they should be out of the house for at least 24 hours. For more specific times, speak with your veterinarian.

** If water by itself will stain a surface that you are treating then a liquid chemical that you mix with water will stain too. For example, water will stain unfinished wood surfaces (cedar walls) and some wall papers. In these situations, use a non-water-based aerosol.

** If you are using a fogging machine (ULD) with an oil base inside, or in an attic or crawlspace under the house, make sure that all sources of heat and flames are turned off or extinguished. Turn off lights, ovens, heaters, pilot lights on gas water heaters (if they are in the area being fogged), and furnaces, air conditioners, and fans.

** Avoid spraying any toys, kitchen utensils, food, etc. You may need to cover these items if you are treating near them or using a fogger. If you accidentally spray any toys or utensils, wash them thoroughly in warm soapy water. If you accidentally spray any food products (human or pet food) promptly dispose of it.

TREATING OUTSIDE

** Avoid any spray drift onto areas that you are not treating, such as ponds, lakes, streams, rivers, flowering plants, gardens, or fruit bearing bushes and fruit trees.

** Avoid spraying any toys, tools, barbecues or barbecue utensils. If you accidentally spray any of these items or other items, wash them thoroughly with soap and water.

** Avoid spraying pet dishes and pet food. If you accidentally spray pet dishes or food you should wash the pet dishes thoroughly in soap and water, and dispose of any food or water that may have been sprayed.

Before attempting to perform any chemical spray inside your home, it is necessary for you to ask everyone that is occupying or visiting if they suffer from allergies or are odor sensitive. If they are, you will want to determine either an alternate way to service the home, or require they be out until all odors have been dispatched.

WHY CONTROL RATS?

There are many reasons we would want to control rats, but the most important reasons I think we should control rats are: Rats contaminate and damage our food, water, and dry goods. Rats can carry disease. Rats can cause electrical fires when they chew on wiring in attics, and wall voids. Rats think of wiring as grass that they can make a nest with. Finally, and probably the most important reason of all, people fear them and lose their feeling of well-being.

About twenty years ago during the winter holidays, my wife Annie had purchased a bag of wild rice for a friend of hers, and had wrapped it up, and put it under our holiday tree. The next day, which was on a Sunday, we were all going out for breakfast, when she noticed wild rice was scattered all around her package. She asked everyone if they had broken the package open, but everyone denied it. After breakfast we came back in, and she went to clean up the spilled rice only to discover there wasn't any rice scattered anymore. She said, "Who cleaned up the rice?" Nobody confessed, so I went over to examine the package and realized that a rat had been chewing on the package. Well, after doing an inspection around the house, I found that our builder had screened our house foundation vents with aluminum screen and the rat had chewed a hole right through one of them, and had come out into the kitchen via one of our base cabinets. I fixed the vent, and because my wife was so stressed from the issue, I set out at least twenty rat traps. The next morning, I had caught the rat. At that time, I realized even though I had been a pest controller for over thirty-two years, I too was very nervous about a rat running loose in my house while we were in bed. There are two kinds of rats, smart, and stupid, or dominant and submissive. The dominant rat always gets the best food, and the best shelter. If you did nothing but set a trap down, you're bound to catch a few stupid ones! If you don't change the environment, the dominants will not be eliminated.

ANTS

Argentine ants, Odorous house ants, Pharaoh ants, Little black house ants, Thief ants, Ghost ants, Carpenter ants, Thatch ants, Pavement ants, Moisture ants (Cornfield ants), Fire ants. All these ants can be controlled by Alpine WSG per label instructions. You should Always use a sprayer that is only used for these products. If you only have one sprayer then triple rinse it with warm water and dish soap, and then rinse with clean water before using this particular pesticide in it. You should never use a bug spray, or bug bomb from the local hardware store when you use this product listed above, as it will negate the effectiveness.

Argentine ants vary in color from light brown to dark brown. Approximately 7 millimeters, or approximately 1/4 inch. They have 2 nodes on the center area (pedicel)

Spread granules on and around mound nest. Or spraying Alpine WSG per label instructions works well.

Odorous house ants are very similar to the Argentine ant except they have only one Node that is more rounded. Use Alpine WSG per label instructions inside and outside.

Pharaoh ants have two nodes and are yellow in color to very light in color. They are approximately 2 millimeters or 1/16 of an inch long. Use Alpine WSG per label instructions inside, and outside as needed.

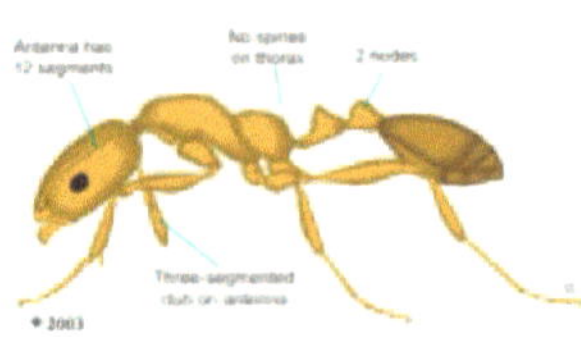

Little black house ants are approximately 2 milliliters long, Black and shiny, and dwell inside walls as well as near water outlets such as kitchen and bathroom sinks. They are omnivores (feed on all different kinds of food) but are especially attracted to sweets. Use Alpine WSG per label instructions in areas of ant traffic. Allow 14 days for control.

Thief ants are very small, approximately 2 milliliters long. They look very similar to the Pharaoh ant, but have different lifestyles when inside a home. They are light in color and have 2 nodes on the pedicel. To control them use Alpine WSG per label instructions wherever they are found. Terro ant gel works well along base boards and backsplashes.

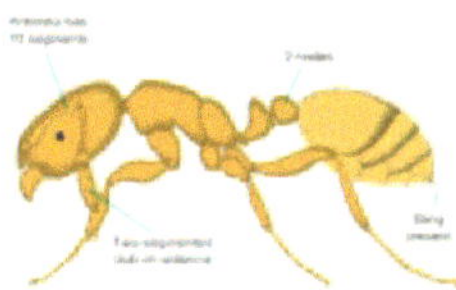

Ghost ants have only one node and a dark head and thorax, with a light brown abdomen. Use Alpine WSG per label instructions in areas you find them.

Carpenter ants have a smooth rounded thorax and a single node. They range from 10 millimeters to as much as 3/4" long. For the most part they infest wood stumps, and house studs and framing. Use Alpine WSG per label instructions outside, and inside. Wall cavities can be injected with Alpine WSG as needed.

Thatch ants build mounds of grass, twigs, and other debris found in the yard. Their nests can be as much as three feet deep under ground. Treat with Alpine WSG per label instructions on the surface, and dig up the debris while treating the ants, larva (little worm like creatures), and eggs.

Thatch ant mounds have eggs and larva in the base of the mound, so it is necessary to dig the mound out completely, saturating the insects and larva as you go. Thatch ants can bite so you should work quickly to avoid being bitten. Use Demand CS per label instructions.

Pavement ants generally live under and between pavements. You can find small mounds of sand or dirt at their entry ways. Use Alpine WSG per label instructions to the cracks where they are trafficking. Try to force the material down through the cracks to reach their nests. The ants are approximately 1/8" in length. Use Alpine WSG on walks that are away from the house as well.

Moisture ants (cornfield ants) These ants feed on rotted vegetation such as harvested corn fields, debris laying on wet soils, in decaying stumps, in shower stalls that have lost the sealing grout between the tiles around a shower stall, concrete wood form boards, and areas wherever there is wood to soil contact with moisture in the wood. You can correct this problem by drying out the wood and treating it with Demand CS per label instructions, then sealing off the leaks that lead to the wood. It may be necessary to remove the bathroom tile to replace the wood members. You may need to contact a licensed contractor for the repairs.

Crazy ants have very long antennae and long legs. They make quick erratic movements. They are reddish brown and are approximately 1/8" long. They can be controlled with Alpine WSG as per label instructions (inside or outside).

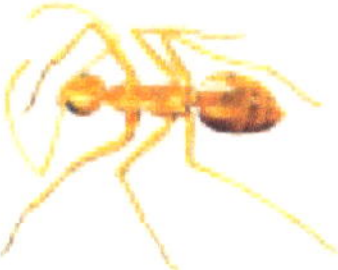

Fire ants get their name by the fiery bite they cause. They range from 1/8" to 1/4" in length. They will build their nests in dry patch areas of the lawn, but will live in any kind of soil. Use Alpine WSG per label instructions. Treat the mounds well to reach down to the actual nest. You can also use fire ant granules to destroy the nest, or Alpine WSG.

Treating mounds with bait granules per label instructions. Spread the granules evenly around the mound. It may take additional treatments if the ants are not foraging for food. You can use Alpine WSG per label instructions, spraying as you dig up the mound, and saturate the nest.

BATS

Bats are feared by most homeowners and the most prevalent bat is called a mouse eared bat. It is dark in color and covered with fur. Large ears and it is rather small like a mouse. Do not pick up a bat that is on the ground as it can be rabid. They are somewhat sluggish during the day and can be removed and disposed of by using a pole and a cardboard glue pad on the end. Simply push the glue board on the bat and it will be stuck on the board and can be safely removed and disposed of. Triple bag it and dispose of it in a dumpster. Sometimes you might find what looks like you have rats on your porch, look for feces generally in the corner of the porch. Where you see the feces, look straight up and you may see feces on the wall. Check the feces by wearing a throw away type glove and roll the feces between your thumb and index finger. If it crumbles, then it is bat feces. Hang a sheet of 6 mil plastic with lathe boards from the top of the porch wall to down at least 5 feet in any areas the bats like to perch. If it is windy, then install some fish weights at the bottom of the plastic sheet. If there are small voids along the ceiling of the porch, they should be either sealed with 1/4" round wood, or seal the opening with caulking.

BEES & WASPS

Honey Bee hives can be found almost anywhere, such as inside a wall of the house, inside the attic, inside an out building, in a meter box, hanging from an eave on the house, or limb of a tree, or even attached to an abandoned automobile, or under a storage building. The first thing to do is to look for their flight pattern going to and from the hive. Once you have located either the actual hive, or if it cannot be found then find the entrance to the hive such as a hole in the wall or compartment opening and apply Delta dust until the hive or opening is covered sufficiently enough to allow the bees to track it in on the hive. If it is not practical to use Delta dust then you can use Wasp and Bee spray in a can. After 2 days go back and check for activity. If possible, remove the hive and any honey found. It may be necessary to hire a contractor that specializes in repairs to put things back the way they were. If you find the bees in a water meter box or an irrigation box, inject into the hole that opens the meter cover with Delta Dust. You can treat either with soapy water on a hanging hive, or wasp and bee spray, or any pesticide labeled for that purpose. Under a storage building, use Demand CS at the entry point, or Delta Dust. After a day or two, return to check if the bees are still actively going into or leaving from the site. You should invest in a bee suit or do the work in the dark of night with a small flashlight turning it on only as needed.

Polistes wasps (paper wasp) build an upside-down nest made of paper they make from shaving particles off from a tree or wood structure. These nests and wasps can be easily sprayed and removed without any protective clothing on as they die very fast using wasp spray from an aerosol can. Simply point and aim and pull the trigger. They will drop immediately and you can scrape off the feather weight like nest. Remove the nest and put in a garbage can. You can deter new nests from forming by using any residual and repellant like spray that has wasps on the label. Be sure to sweep up the dead wasp so that pets will not eat them and receive venom.

Mud Dauber wasps are somewhat docile and solitary, however they can be frightening because of their size. Simply spray with a wasp and bee spray aerosol can once. Then with a putty knife remove the nest and place in the garbage. You can deter new nests from forming by using any residual and repellant spray that has wasps on the label.

Bees and Wasps This includes the following: Honey bees (Killer bees Africanized bees), Yellow Jackets, Bumble bees, Hornets, Mud dauber wasps, and Polistes wasps. The best way to eliminate these insects is to treat the nest directly, if possible.

Honey bees are a social animal which means they all live in a group and work together with their own individual duties. The queen starts out together with a male and is inseminated by him, and she then begins to lay eggs for her first brood of workers. The male eventually leaves and dies. The first eggs hatch and become larvae and are fed by the queen with her existing nourishment in her body. They then transform into pupae in a silken case, then through metamorphosis they physically change into adults. Because they are only nourished by the queen's own nourishment in her body, they come out smaller than a normal size. Some of them become workers and forage to provide food for the new growing colony. Some of them become hive builders, and some are soldiers to protect the group from outsiders, and some become nurse maids to take care of the larvae while they are maturing. After a period of time, the queen produces royal eggs which can potentially become new kings and queens that eventually leave the hive to make new colonies. If you approach honey bees on bushes or flowers, they are foraging for food or building materials for the hive. They are not a threat to you as long as they are not at the hive location. If you approach a hive they can be very aggressive as they think you are a threat to the queen. If you are trying to control a swarm but it is in an isolated area where there is no imminent danger to people around, you can leave the swarm and it will leave on its own accord when the queen has rested and may leave an hour or two later or maybe as long as a day later, however if you want it eliminated regardless of the danger then proceed with caution.

Honey bee

Bee swarm

Comb (hive)

The first thing that I recommend is that a drop cloth or bucket be set under the swarm before you spray to prevent any dogs or cats in the area from trying to eat the bees, which can be toxic to them. Upon completion of the treatment clean up any bees that are left on the ground. The second step is to mix up one cup of liquid dish soap with one gallon of water. Put on a bee outfit that will protect you from the bees stinging when you apply the solution to the swarm. Using a clean hand can pump up sprayer, gently spray with a fan tip or cone nose orifice all around the outside layer of the swarm. Wait a minute and then spray it again only with more force until the bees drop off. Continue to spray the swarm all around it until all of the bees have dropped off. If the swarm has been eliminated and you still have a few bees flying around, don't worry as the queen is dead and the left over bees will die without any more activity. A swarm can be found on a tree limb or on the side of a house or simply on the ground. The procedure is basically the same but be sure the bees are dead and cleaned up. There may be some returning and flying around the area where the swarm was, but don't worry about it. Stay away from the area until they are all gone.

BEE AND WASP PROTECTIVE CLOTHING

Don't take chances; wear the protective clothing, or do it in the dark at night.

BEDBUGS

Always follow the Pesticide label, as it is the law.

Bedbugs are blood feeders. With the modernization of travel and the improvement of roads throughout the United Sates, our country has become very mobile. Bedbugs can be brought into your state by means of hitching a ride in moving vans, cars, motor homes, trains, buses, suitcases and any cargo that is shipped in freight, including passenger airlines. With this in mind we must look at the possibility that any Bedbugs that are out there surely can be found anywhere in the USA including your own state. Bedbugs require a blood meal, but can go without eating for up to 6 months. They have a simple life cycle. They lay their eggs in undisturbed areas, and once the eggs have hatched they become nymphs (young adults). While they are growing larger, it is important that they have a blood meal to grow to the next size. As an adult they are approximately 3/16" long and are reddish brown with an oval shape. They are not known to carry disease; however, they can cause irritating itching that when their bite is scratched can lead to bacteria causing an additional infection. To correct the infestation you must first take all the clothes and bedding in that room and wash and dry them after the treatment is done. Start to treat the seams of the mattress with Bedlam from an aerosol can. Treat in the corners of the ceiling with the same product. Spray with Bedlam in cracks along window and door frames, closet rails and any other areas such as bathrooms in the same bedroom. Remove all items from the bathroom and store in sealed plastic bags. Next step is to treat the box springs that hold the mattress in place. Lift the box springs up on one side on its end and insert small slits in the underside through the dust screen, then inject a wide cone spray throughout the interior of the box spring using Demand CS at a maximum rate allowable by the label. You will want to spray with Bedlam in a can behind pictures hanging on the walls, then treat the bed frame at all cracks and crevices along with the headboard. If there is carpet secured at the baseboards, you should treat as a crack and crevice method making sure to spray enough material with the Demand CS to reach down behind the tack strip. After the bed and frame are complete, the next item to do is to treat inside and outside cracks of the dresser and nightstand, as well as any other furniture in the room at all cracks and crevices using either Bedlam and or Demand CS. After all the rooms that are infected are treated, treat the davenports, footrests, and other upholstered furniture with Bedlam in all the tufts of the furniture as a crack and crevice treatment. Be sure to extinguish any flame like gas stoves, hot water tanks, and portable heaters that are in the house. Turn off any AC unit thermostats. There is no need to treat the garage unless Bedbugs have been found there. The final step is to use a canister of Pyrethrum and spray around the room to eliminate bedbugs that may be still in the rooms that you did not see before. You should have the house ventilated for 2 to 4 hours minimum when you return.

The house should have all people and pets removed for these treatments and well ventilated before re-entry.

Adult Bedbug

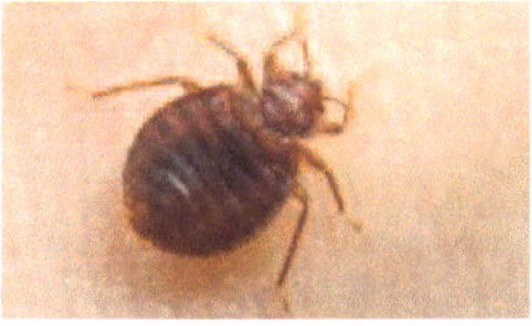

Bedbug bites on skin

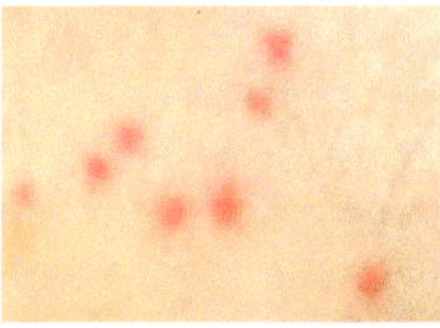

BAT BUG

Always follow the Pesticide label, as it is the law.

Bed Bug (Cimex Lectularius) **Bat bug** (Cimex Adjunctus)

Bat Bug

The first important thing to look at is where are most of the Bedbugs found? Bedbugs will be more in the lower areas of a room such as baseboards, closet floors, bedding, bed frames, and dresser drawers. The Batbugs are found in most cases around ceiling fixtures, ceiling vents, and other items that are mainly high on the walls, or ceiling. Bats can be accessing the attic and the Batbugs with them are venturing away from the bats in search of more hosts. If they are Batbugs you will need to check the attic roof for roof accesses and treat with a dust such as Delta dust in the attic or voids such as cathedral ceilings. You will also want to treat the rooms below the same as though they were Bedbugs.

DARKLING BEETLE

There are over 20,000 different species of Darkling Beetles throughout the world. Darkling Beetles do not fly as their wings are fused together. The larva stage of the beetle is called a Mealworm. They feed on grain, and any decaying animal or plant matter. They have a complete life cycle (egg, larva, pupa, adult). They are nocturnal spending their time in activity during the night. Some of the Darkling Beetles can live 3 to 4 months while other species can live up to 10 years. They are considered a nuisance pest but do not harm people or pets. The use of Demand

CS at maximum allowable rate around the foundation, and eliminating decaying matter such as mulch and decaying wood piles at the same area will greatly reduce the populations.

Occasional invaders

BEETLES

Ladybird beetle

This beetle is commonly called a Ladybug. It is a good insect to have in your garden as it eats other harmful insects that attack different plants, however in large numbers it can be a nuisance to people. In the winter they can over winter in crawlspaces under the house and in attics, and wall voids. In the spring they can come up through the floors where there are openings such as heat registers and overhead recessed lighting. Using pyrethrum sprays in canisters or fogging machines for large voids under the house or attics you can treat to eliminate the populations. If they are in wall voids you can drill 1/8-inch holes between the wall studs and inject pyrethrum from a canister that has an injection needle.

BIRDS

Pigeons (Rock Doves)

Always follow the Pesticide label, as it is the law.

Pigeons can be controlled in many ways depending on where they are nesting or just loafing (visiting).

1. Netting them off of an area.
2. Using ledge sliders.
3. Trapping with cages.
4. Toxic feeders (should only be used in areas that are inaccessible to children and pets.) Use Avitrol with corn 1 to 19 parts, in a dormer feeder with 1/8" mesh on the bottom of the feeder. Be sure to attach bottom of feeder with screws into inserts on the roof tile or other roofing materials, and a place where there would be no chance of the corn coming off the roof.

Pigeons can carry disease and parasites of which it is important to disinfect the area where they are nesting. You should clean up any area that has feces dropped by them. Pigeons can be deterred by loud sounds of distressed birds, or plastic owls, or fake snakes, but can only work for a short time before they realized that the sound, or fake predator item is not a threat to them.

Bird Control

The two most common pest birds are the Starlings, and Pigeons. They are not protected as of this date, but that can change later down the road. It is always important to check with the local wildlife authorities before you do anything to be sure the particular birds you are trying to control are not protected.

Starlings have long beaks and various colors on a generally dark brown body. They can make various sounds such as imitating other birds and animals. For the most part we find them living in areas that have openings they can access such as bird block vents that are at the eaves of a roof line. The easiest method of control is to wait for them to fly out of the access, then screen off the opening with 1/4" galvanized steel screen.

Bird Block vents

Bird Control
Pigeons

Netting off areas that Pigeons nest

First locate the nesting areas, and remove nests and clean the areas. Disinfect the areas with simple green, sterifab, or any cleaning material that will kill bacteria or virus. Next drill holes with a 3/16-inch masonry bit for a tile roof, or for a composition, or wood shingle roof use screws and sealant approximately every 6 inches along where you want the net to be. Next for tile roofs install plastic inserts and eye screws with a sealant. Next run a 1/8-inch stainless cable around through the eye bolts. (If the tile is Spanish tile, make sure there is an eye bolt in the lower part of the tile to prevent the birds from going under the cable.) Next install a 4-inch turnbuckle using ferrule clamps to the cable. Next, using 2-inch black colored bird netting, attach the netting to the cable with hog rings.

Turnbuckle

Hog ring applicator

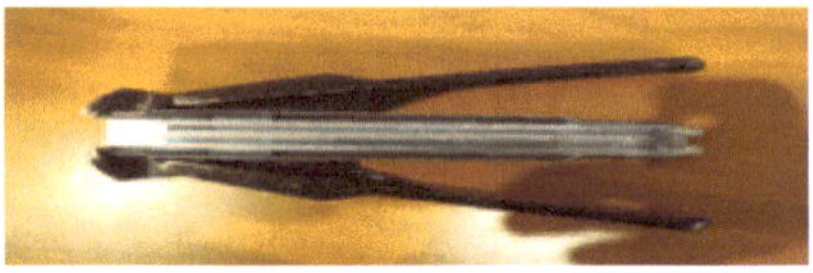

The pictures below are of bird dormer vent feeders which should only be used for loafing pigeons. (These are non-nesters, just visiting pigeons.) Install a 1/8" or smaller screen that will drain any rain that gets into it. It should be placed on the roof dormer vent bottom, and install the bottom of the dormer vent to the tile roof, or any shingle roof with inserts, screws and sealant. Place Avitrol whole corn bait at the ratio of one part Avitrol to 5 to 19 parts clean non poisoned whole corn. This station should be left on the roof for as long as needed to stop loafing pigeons from roosting. Caution should be taken to prevent any corn from falling off the roof. Upon the completion of the work, the remaining corn and Avitrol needs to be removed. As per the label the corn and Avitrol should be installed in the morning and removed at the end of the day. Install a mirror inside of the front of the dormer vent to make a pigeon think another bird is in there.

FABRIC PESTS

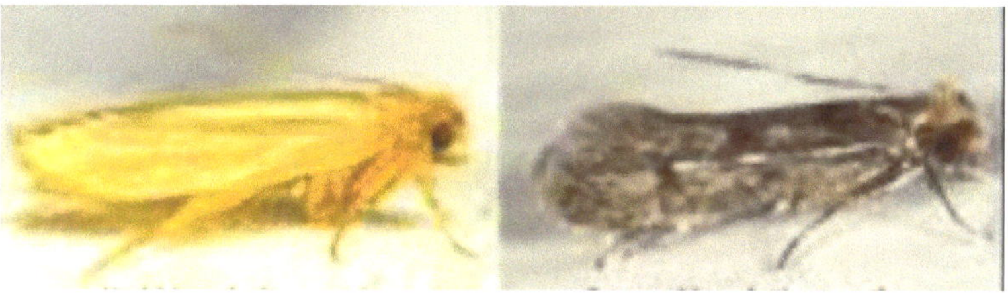

Webbing Clothes Moth

Always follow the Pesticide label, as it is the law.

The Webbing Clothes Moth is the most common fabric damaging moth in the state. It has a golden color to its wings, with a fringe of hair along the ends of the wings. This moth is rather small in comparison to other moths. It is approximately 3/8 inch in length. This moth shuns light and can be found generally in closets, that are undisturbed, or in boxes or chests that have woolen fabrics that have been stored for 2 plus years. To correct this infestation, it is necessary to remove all the items and either have the stored items fumigated such as in garbage bags with a Dichlorvos strip in a glass jar with a lid and holes approximately 1/8th inch in the lid for at least 72 hours, or wash and dry clean the items that cannot be washed, and the storage container should be (depending on whether it will not stain the container) sprayed with a pyrethrum-based spray.

Case Making Moth

The Case Making Moth has spots on its forewings that if examined closely can be seen but sometimes very light. The Case Making Moth is smaller than the Webbing Clothes Moth. The Case Making Moth is around 1/4" in length, and is a mixture of brown and gray on the wings. When the larva stage develop, they spin a silken sack that they carry along until it is ready to go into the pupa stage. The sack is then completed and closes the larva inside while it is developing into the adult moth. This sack is covered with the same fibers that the larva is feeding on, so it is sometimes hard to see. The food source can be any item that is natural, or has been soiled with natural material such as skin, food, etc. Follow the same corrective procedure that the Webbing Clothes Moth has.

Carpet beetles are often found on windowsills and in clothing such as any natural substance material like wool, leather, items made from feathers, mounted animal heads, dead rodents, and clothes that are synthetic but have been soiled, and other places that have deposited natural things such as skin that comes off a person's body. (We get a new set of skin on our bodies approximately every 30 days.) Carpeting, throw rugs, food like oatmeal, grains, wheat that have been opened but not used for 6 months or longer. Dried fruit, nuts, and dog or cat food containers that have been opened but not used up and have been left for 6 months or more. When carpet beetles have been discovered you should determine if you have, or had a rodent problem in the past. It can be the source of the infestation from either the poison bait that was not finished by the rodents, or the carpet beetle is living off the carcass of the dead rodents. If you have, then see my section on rodent correction. You should check the clothes closet for evidence of feeding on wool suits, or any clothes that have been worn and not been cleaned yet. Wool or items that have been soiled with organic substances and put away in boxes or dresser cabinets should be checked for any evidence of the carpet beetle. Treatment should be targeted to cracks and crevices only as the carpet beetles will not be in an open area such as the middle of a room. You will want to treat all the baseboards throughout the house and all the cracks and crevices in areas that are not disturbed very often. Treat the joint between the carpet and tile floor. If you find evidence of them in food cabinets such as wheat products, you can super heat the food (20 minutes in the oven at 140 degrees), or simply throw the infected food out.

Preparation required before treatment

1. Move items away from the walls about 6 inches except large heavy furniture.
2. Move items away from the walls in the closets such as shoes, shoe boxes, toys, etc.
3. Check any stored clothes for evidence of the carpet beetles.
4. Check any hanging clothes for evidence of them as well.
5. Turn off any fish air intake tubes and place above the treated baseboards at least 2 feet up from the baseboards. Cover tank(s)

with a cloth, or plastic sheet, or newspaper.
6. Children (babies, toddlers, and all pets) should be removed from the house for a minimum of 2 to 4 hours, and if the pets or children have a respiratory condition they should be out for a minimum of 24 to 48 hours.
7. Treat with a heavy crack and crevice stream all baseboards throughout the house. Use aerosols that have the correct label on any furniture that is infested.
8. Clothing that is infected should be cleaned.
9. Any trophy heads that are infected should be treated by fumigation, such as Vapona strips placed in large bags containing the trophy heads. They should be kept in the bags and sealed with tie straps at least 48 hours. Then remove them from the bag to be placed where they can be on display.

Varied Carpet Beetle

Black Furniture Beetle

COCKROACHES

There are many kinds of cockroaches throughout the world, and quite notably they can carry many diseases that plague mankind, such as Leprosy, food poisoning, Urinary tract infections, Gastroenteritis, Gas gangrene, Diarrhea, Pneumonia, and Actinomycetoma. These problems can be avoided by eliminating the cockroaches from the home or restaurants, or commercial establishments. The most common cockroach is the German Cockroach. This roach is from the tropical areas of the world and have spread out by commerce throughout the planet. It thrives in moist areas such as kitchens, bathrooms, food preparation areas and wherever moisture occurs inside of a dwelling. The German roach does not fare well outside due to the temperatures and dry areas found outside. Preparation for treatment should include all kitchen or food preparation areas should be void of dishes, pots, pans and food items. Nothing should be left in cabinets, counter tops, sinks, drawers prior to treatment. If items are left on the kitchen table and covered, they will be okay. All baseboards throughout the dwelling should be clear of toys, shoes, pet dishes, magazines, etc. All pets and aquariums should be contained or removed. Air supply should be turned off and aquariums covered. Treat with Alpine WSG for best results using a sprayer devoted to only non-repellant products. Use max rate on label but no higher. You should allow all surfaces to dry that have been treated before you allow anyone to occupy the room(s). Any person or animal that has respiratory or allergic reaction to chemical should be out for 24 to 48 hours. Things can be put back after dry time of at least 2 to 4 hours. Shelf paper can be used but to not wash counter tops or cabinet drawers or cabinets until roaches have been eliminated.

Turkistan Roach, and Oriental Roach

These roaches are not an inside roach, but tend to be near water such as pools, and irrigation boxes. If you see them inside the dwelling, it is just an accidental entry. Spray the exterior perimeter of the dwelling and inside the irrigation boxes outside with Demand CS at the maximum rate: .06%

German Cockroach

Turkistan

Oriental

CRICKETS

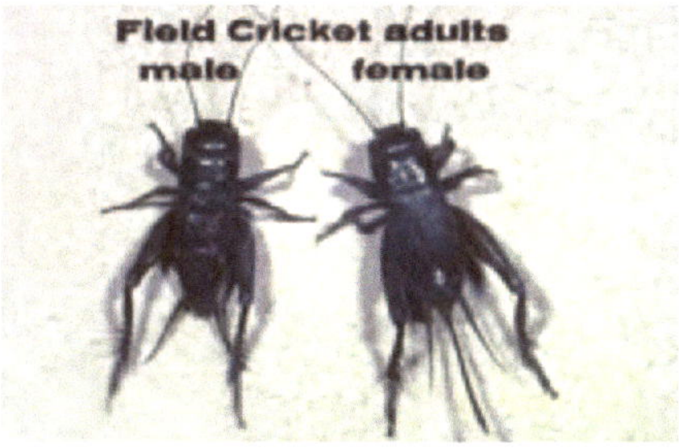

Field Crickets live under rocks, fallen trees, tall grass, and under firewood for the most part. They require fresh water so they will most likely be found around pet water dishes, or over watered plants and grass. They can jump approximately 3 feet away when disturbed. When you hear their chirping it is the male rubbing its wings to attract a female. They are nocturnal and are attracted to lights at night. During the day they will stay hidden under foliage. They have a simple metamorphosis as egg, nymph, adult. The cricket lives on an average of about 3 months. They hatch from an egg in the spring and as a full-grown insect are anywhere from 1/2" to 1" in body length. If they access the house they can feed on cotton, wool, silk, and fur. They can and do carry disease that can be transferred to humans but it is not life threatening. Full grown crickets can bite but they only do so when handled. Use Demand CS at max rate sprayed where they are found. Generally around the foundation of a house or building and along baseboards inside when found there. Sometimes they will be living inside the hollow void of the garage walls. Injecting with Demand CS at the maximum rate of .06% between each wall stud, and from the outside treat up on the underside of the siding will fix the problem.

Jerusalem Cricket

The Jerusalem Cricket average size you will encounter is approximately 2 inches in length. This cricket is omnivorous, (eats meat, fruit, and vegetables). This cricket climbs well but cannot fly. It will bite humans, but only when threatened. Its life span is approximately 6 months then mate, and then dies. This cricket lives for the most part underground, however during mating season will stay above the ground. The area around the house foundation should be treated up 3 feet on the siding and concrete foundation with Demand CS at the maximum rate of .06% with water as the carrying base.

FLEAS

Fleas originate from the outside. When a flea becomes an adult, it begins to look for a host. After a flea has found a host they stay on the host, feed on the blood, and lay eggs for the rest of their adult life, which is about 2 to 3 weeks. The eggs are non-sticky and fall off the host onto the floor or ground. In a few days they will hatch into the larval stage. All flea stages can be found throughout the house but the majority of the population is located where the hosts (pets) spend most of their time. When treating for fleas, you should treat all floor surfaces inside the dwelling, being sure to check under furniture cushions, and lightly treat those areas with an insect growth regulator such as Precor 2000 that has an adulticide as well in it. Using Demand CS at the rate of .03% mixed with water, treat the yard outside to approximately 10 feet, and other areas that the pets frequent outside such as dog runs to make sure you get complete control of the situation.

Recommended Preparation Before Treating for Fleas

Vacuum under cushions of the sofa and cushioned chairs, along baseboards, the entire carpeted areas and around the pet bed areas and wash any pet bedding. Place a Vapona strip inside the vacuum to kill the adult fleas that have been vacuumed. Empty the vacuum into the garbage. Pick up everything off of the floor or ground (inside and outside) that is not furniture or rugs. Example: magazines, toys, shoes, pet dishes, etc. It is not necessary to move dog houses or plants, and do not stack items on couch or upholstered chairs because they will be treated. Flip up bedspreads so you can treat under the bed, and walk-in closets or closets that the pet enters will also be treated. In those areas pick up shoes and long dresses or clothes off of the floor. Cover fish tanks and turn off any air pumps. Raise pump air intake tubes above floor at least two feet off the floor. Remove all birds for a minimum of 24 hours. All other pets should be out until house floors are dry and the house has been ventilated well. Plan to be out of the house 2 to 4 hours to allow ample time for surfaces to dry. It is recommended that the pet be treated or bathed for fleas the same day. You should Vacuum all carpeting upon returning. If you or others have allergies, you or others should vacate until the house has been well ventilated. Vacuuming on your return will stimulate the adult fleas to hatch out of the pupa stage and come in contact with the recently treated surfaces. Use an adulticide and an IGR (Insect growth regulator). Spray any dog runs and dog houses outside. Caution should be observed to only use aerosol cans of spray for furniture to avoid stains on the wood portions and cloth portions. Avoid spraying wallpaper and wood walls as this can stain them. Be careful to spray lightly on dark colored surfaces to avoid activating any wax that is on the floor or furniture. Automobiles that transport the animals should also be treated with a flea aerosol such as Precor 2000 that has both an adulticide as well as an insect growth regulator. Be sure that the vehicle is not used until completely dry inside as well as ventilated.

Fleas

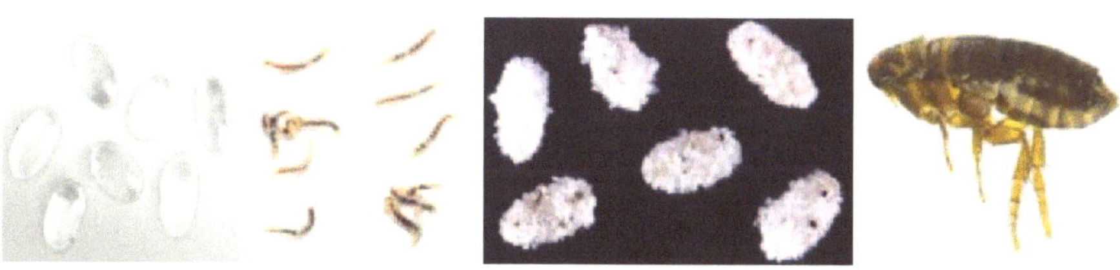

Eggs **Larva** **Pupae** **Adult**

FLIES

Phorid Fly or Humpback Fly

Always follow the Pesticide label, as it is the law.
This fly is approximately 1/16 inch in size and has gray to brown eyes. They are attracted to stagnated water. Look for signs of a plumbing leak or water line that is broken coming from the street. Look for standing water in a crawlspace or moist soils in the crawlspace. This fly is attracted by moist decaying matter. Check roof gutters for built up silt. Check for water-logged gardens or your yard. The correction is to eliminate the stagnant water. Aerosol fogging will give some relief as will electric Fly Light Traps. It is a slow process to correct the problem because it may take several months to dry out an area. Often corrective measures such as putting pea-gravel in the crawlspace with a vapor barrier over it. Ventilate crawlspace. Check the water meter when all known outlets are turned off. If all the fixtures are off and the meter is still running then there is a leak somewhere in the pipes that needs to be repaired.

Marsh Fly

There are several species of this fly throughout the world. This fly is common in your area. Its larvae are aquatic and have a complete life cycle. The Larvae feed on slugs and snails going through their molting. They are found wherever water is abundant such as ponds, slow moving rivers, swimming pools, and over watered lawns. Keeping swimming pools chlorinated and preventing foliage from being over watered is the best method of control.

Having said this, sometimes the numbers are so great that they will sit on your house siding during the daytime for the warmth. You can spray the siding to eliminate the current flies.

Midges

Midges are similar in appearance and size as a mosquito but without the long proboscis (long sucking mouth part) found on mosquitoes. Midges are aquatic during the larva stage and the adults are attracted to moist conditions. They are night flyers and attracted to light. The midges we have in your area do not bite. When they are seen it is generally in very large numbers. Their life spans are from one to two weeks. The correct method would be using a heavy fogging machine outside where they are. The chemical of choice is Pyrethrum such as BP100. For better long-lasting control, keep the moisture down on foliage and keep the water in the pool properly cleaned and maintain the correct level of chlorine in the pool.

Drain Fly

Drain flies often breed in floor drains, sink drains, bathtub drains, and shower drains. Their breeding can be found in areas of water with bacteria buildup. These flies can carry and transmit diseases as a result of being in sewage drains. This fly is approximately 2 centimeters long (1/13th inch long) Their wings are heavily coated with hairs that make them appear to be moths, they are sometimes referred to as a moth fly. They are attracted to lights inside of a house at night, and can be found on windowsills. Most of the breeding takes place in the fall of the year. The method of correction is to place a drain moth pesticide called Bio-Gel in all your drain accesses. This will remove the scum built up in the drains which they feed on.

Fungus Gnat

These gnats are very small, approximately 1/16 to 1/8 inch, and can be identified by their dark grey wings. They live approximately 30 days. They generally breed in rotting and moist soil either in an atrium or plant pot. Turning the soil and drying it out, and using less water, and less frequent watering can help with the control. This Gnat feeds on fungus and if the fungus can be eliminated so will the Gnat. Control them with white vinegar and a small amount of dish soap. Placing small rocks on top of the soil will help as well.

House fly

This fly is one of the most common flies in a house. This fly is approximately 1/4 inch in length and the thorax has 4 distinct dark lines running down from the head to the abdomen. Dog feces are one of the most common food sources outside the house for this fly. It is important to remember that the feces should be policed up each day to lessen the problem inside. Other sources such as fermenting garbage in the kitchen and compost piles outside should be looked at as a source as well. This fly can carry several diseases such as Cholera, diarrhea, dysentery, tuberculosis, and ophthalmic as well as parasitic worms. The cure can be obtained by using sanitation methods, and spraying the infected areas outside and using an aerosol spray inside. Screens on the doors and windows will help and keeping doors and windows closed when not in use. If you want a quick relief then a temporary solution would be to use a fly trap machine, or an organic trap seen on the right.

This fly goes by all these names.

Fannia or Lesser house fly, or little house fly

This fly is approximately 3/16" long. It has 3 dark lines on its thorax that run to the start of the abdomen. They seldom rest on surfaces and fly aimlessly around the center of a room. This fly can cause intestinal myiasis in humans, and occasionally may pass harmful pathogens to man. They have been found feeding on stored bacon, dried fish, and fecal from various livestock. They also can be found around garbage cans and compost piles. Use the same procedures that are used for the house fly.

Cluster fly

This fly over winters in a void such as a wall of a house, or an attic in the late summer or early fall. In the springtime it lays its eggs in the ground at a grassy area where early grubs, worms, or beetle larva are present. The egg hatches on the larva or worm and immediately burrows into the subject and starts to feed from the inside out. Once the larva or worm is dead, the larva pupates in the soil and becomes a cluster fly. This procedure continues each year until the grass has been treated with an insecticide that kills the larvae for the next cycle in the next year. Identification is the wings are closed at the tips and golden (yellow) hairs are on the thorax section. For a temporary fix of the problem you can treat the attic with Pyrethrum with a fogger and treat with a pyrethrum material that is in a compressed air can under the base of the exterior siding wall area. The cluster fly is not considered as a filth fly nor does it spread disease, however they can be quite a nuisance in large numbers in the house.

Fruit Fly

Fruit Flies are very small flies with large red eyes. This fly is approximately 1/8 of an inch long. Fruit flies are a common pest in households and restaurants, they are attracted to fresh fruits or fermenting fruit and vegetables. They lay their eggs near or on the surface of fermenting materials. Other sources include dishwater in sinks, sour mops, or drain pans under refrigerators, floor drains, and excess slop water that seeps into cracks and crevices under baseboards and other places when scrubbing the floors. These sources contain small particles of food that make them a perfect place for fruit flies to breed. Seeing fruit flies inside is usually a definite sign that there is some fermenting material nearby. The use of Bio-Gel in the floor drains works well to eliminate the fermenting food materials. The most effective way to eliminate the flies is to find what they are breeding in, or attracted to, and throw it out. Usually it is a piece of fruit or garbage that just missed the garbage can. Glue boards with a few drops of vinegar work well to attract and trap fruit flies. The use of aerosol canisters with pyrethrum works well. Be sure to clean up the material they are breeding in as well.

Bottle flies

These flies can be Black, Blue and Green metallic flies. These flies are large robust metallic looking flies. They all lay their eggs in the eyes of a dead carcass such as but not limited to dead rodents, birds, etc. On occasion they will also lay eggs in fermenting garbage. Bottle flies are a signal that something else is wrong such as an ingression of unwanted animals in the attic or crawlspace that have died. Check both areas and when you find the source, remove it and disinfect the location with DSV, or Bac-A-Zap

IMP AND RODENTS

This section of the book is on commensal rodents. Commensal rodents are rodents that share our dinner table with us, because man is the only animal on earth that wastes food. If we purchase and open a product that is to be refrigerated, but fail to consume it, most of us throw it away in two to three weeks whether it is bad or not. All other animals would consume it in any state of its freshness.

When I was a young boy, my father would take me on his pest control route on Saturdays, and on days that he would do rodent work I would help him carry his box of bait and on occasion he would have me pick up and refresh the bait in the boxes that were used back then. Most of them were homemade of wood, and some were made of prefabricated cardboard that he would buy from his suppliers. This was a few years before EPA existed, and before there were any real government standards that the pest control companies had to follow. Back then everyone essentially made up the procedures as they went along. Speaking from the experience I have had over the years, I would say we have come a long way in truly protecting our environment, and reducing unnecessary risks that our forefathers dealt with. As I got into my twenties I became very active in pest control with my uncle who also owned a company. Shortly after I went to work for him, he passed away, and I purchased the business from his estate. That was fifty-four years ago. One of the problems that always bothered me was many of the companies baited with poison in attics, crawlspaces, and inside the garages, and even inside the kitchen. I know a lot of the time one can get lucky and nothing becomes of this practice, but sometimes it can backfire and a rodent will die under a kitchen cabinet, or in a wall or in the ceiling between floors. This can lead to a horrible smell and a fly problem and an unhappy customer. In the '70s I happened to pick up a state pest control manual that explained IPM (Integrated Pest Management). Its approach was very simple. It described how you could change the environment so the rodents will not be interested in the area and would leave on their own accord. IPM meant closing off openings, and changing the environment made total sense to me, so I began to approach the problem with that in mind.

IPM

IPM stands for Integrated Pest Management. IPM is controlling pests with more than just toxicants, such as using mechanical devices, removing harborage sites, eliminating food and water sources, and changing the environment to be less attractive to pests.

I started learning about IPM at a very early age. When I was sixteen years old, my father had been a pest controller for about ten years at that time. One day, Dad and I were in the backyard at our home talking, when all of a sudden, he saw a rat in our yard. A four-foot chain link fence enclosed our yard. Just about the time he saw the rat, I saw it too. Immediately my father took chase, with me right on his heels. The rat knew he was in serious trouble, so he bolted across the yard, with Dad and myself in hot pursuit. Just as the rat reached the fence he ran right through it. Dad having anticipated the fence was already in the air jumping and clearing the fence by an easy margin. When he landed, by just pure luck, he landed on top of the rat. Dad turned to me with a grin, and said, "Son that's one dead rat!" That's IPM.

Another example of IPM happened after I was in the business for about ten years. I got a call from an elderly lady who must have been in her eighties. She told me that she had a big rat in her desk at home, and wanted me to remove it. I thought she was crazy, but I wasn't very busy that day so I agreed to come out and if nothing else, show her she was wrong. When I arrived and introduced myself, she brought me to the desk, and said, "The rat is in this top drawer." I slowly opened the drawer only to expose the backend of a very large rat. I was in total shock. Incidentally, that's when I discovered that if the rat can't see you, he thinks you can't see him either. I told the lady that she and her husband would need to leave the house so I could work without them being in my way. They left, and then I went out to my truck and got an ice pick, and a broom handle, and secured the ice pick to the end of the handle. I then went over to the desk and carefully opened the drawer. The rat was out so fast, I didn't even get a good look at him. Over the next hour I was chasing the rat from room to room, knocking lamps over, and turning furniture upside down. I finally took my shirt off because of all the sweating. After a few more minutes the rat came wobbling out from under a recliner chair, and then with all the energy I could muster I nailed the rat. That's IPM.

MOSQUITOES

Always follow the Pesticide label, as it is the law.

The two most encountered mosquitoes in our area are the Aedes and the Culex mosquitoes. Both of these are a serious threat to our health and well-being. The Aedes carries the Zika virus, and the Culex carries the West Nile virus. Both of the mosquitoes are aquatic in the larva stage. They can breed in unclean swimming pools that are rarely serviced. They also can breed in any body of water that is stagnant such as a pond or an irrigation ditch. During the night and at dusk they are most active feeding on blood from people and animals. During the daytime they are resting in any sheltered area such as dry culverts, rockeries, hollow logs, and tall grass or weeds. To control them it is important to change their breeding by maintaining swimming pool cleanliness and using chlorine or even liquid soap in any stagnant water. There are other control chemicals such as abacus briquettes from a pesticide supplier. The use of a repellant on people such as DEET can be helpful. The scientist say that the mosquitoes prefer type O blood, as opposed to type A and B blood. Female mosquitoes need a blood meal to lay eggs. Male mosquitoes feed on plant nectar as opposed to blood.

Aedes albopictus **Culex nigripalpus**

OCCASIONAL INVADERS

Always follow the Pesticide label, as it is the law.

Silverfish **Firebrats**

Silverfish are somewhat flattened and gray to silver in color, and firebrats are more brownish and have a hump on their back. They can be found throughout the house including living rooms, bedrooms, bathrooms, kitchens, garages and even attics. However, they usually prefer warm areas like furnace rooms, hot water tank rooms, and areas near skylights. They are defined as a paper product pest because they will often attack and eat away old books, magazines, maps, and even fallen hair from our bodies. Barber shops can also have this pest as a result of hair left in cracks and crevices. They have also been found attacking fabrics such as cotton and linen. Usually they enter buildings via cardboard boxes, books or papers, which are brought in from infested areas, however, they can also enter structures directly from the outside. During the daytime they usually prefer to hide in small cracks and crevices. When searching for food they can roam quite some distance, although when a good food source is found they will usually remain nearby. They can live inside walls as well, and especially an exterior wall. Dusting wall voids with Silica jell or Drione will fix it. To eliminate them from rooms and outside you can use Bifenthrin along baseboards inside, and along the foundation outside.

Centipede

Millipede

Always follow the Pesticide label, as it is the law.

All of these arthropods are associated with moisture. They are all found in and around high moisture areas such as piles of leaves, loose bark, in rotting logs, under rocks, grass clippings, and mulch. In some cases they can infest homes thus becoming a nuisance. Inside, they are usually found in damp basements, bathrooms, closets or near potted plants. Eliminating their sources of harborage is a key element in eliminating and preventing an infestation. Over watering the flower beds outside of entry areas to the house can also trigger infestations. These arthropods can inflict pain on your skin. I do not recommend you handle them without some kind of prong for capturing them. Drying out the area is recommended, and using an insecticide such as Demand CS at max rate, that will prevent them from returning can help. Installing round half-inch aggregate on top of soil areas along the exterior of the foundations such as sliders and doors will help.

Earwig

Sow Bug

BOOK LICE OR PSOCIDS

Always follow the Pesticide label, as it is the law.

Most Psocids or Book lice can be found in the indoor areas. They can breed in damp locations such as around water areas like leaky plumbing pipes or on overwatered house plants. They do not bite, however they can become a nuisance when in large numbers. They feed on mold and sometimes are found on bookshelves, in old books that have mold on the pages because of the lack of fresh air. To correct the problem, the area that they are found in should be dried, and use of Silica Jell in the area. Fixing any plumbing leaks if they exist is also a good remedy. These insects are very small, approximately 1/32 of an inch. Translucent to gray in color.

SPRINGTAIL INSECT

Springtails are not a serious problem but they can be a nuisance. These small insects (approximately 1/16 of an inch) are a problem when they are in large numbers. Getting rid of springtails requires finding any moist areas of the house such as under a sink with a leak or overwatered house plants. Pyrethrum sprayed on to the soil of house plants will help to keep the numbers down. You can as an alternative take some of the topsoil of the planter out, and replace it with a layer of pea gravel. These insects can be dark brown, or translucent in color. Springtails are wingless insects that are about 1/16 inch long. They have a tail-like appendage underneath their body and when disturbed use this tail to propel themselves 3 to 4 inches into the air. Springtails lay their eggs grouped together in moist soil, are typically harmless and feed on decaying organic matter. When checking out the problem, look for mold or fungi which they feed on.

FALSE CHINCH BUG

Always follow the Pesticide label, as it is the law.

False Chinch Bugs can get up to approximately 1/4" in length and they enjoy and thrive in hot and dry areas, especially near vegetation. For the most part they do not cause significant damage to foliage. When they become massive in numbers the spot areas that they thrive in can be treated with Demand CS per label instructions. They do not bite. Their eggs are generally laid at the base of plants outside. They have a simple metamorphosis. They can be found around sprinkler heads and leaky water hoses.

CONENOSE, KISSING BUG, ALSO CALLED ASSASSIN BUG

Chagas Disease is a direct cause of a bite by the Conenose or Kissing Bug. This disease can cause heart disease in people. This insect is a blood piercing and sucking animal that can infect the host with serious consequences. Conenose Bugs can hide inside a home in furniture or cracks in the floor or bed frames. These insects generally attack people by biting them on the face at night. Treating the inside of the house at all cracks of the home with Demand CS can eliminate them.

CICADAS

Adult

Nymph shedding outer skeleton

Cicadas live underground from 13 to 17 years and then emerge from the soil leaving a round hole approximately 1/2" to 3/4" as they come out. They have large bright orange eyes and are approximately 3/4" long. They come out in the springtime and find a tree or fence to climb up on and shed their outer skeleton covering. They at that time have wings and the males make a mating call for the females. After mating, the females puncture a hole into the limbs of a tree and lay hundreds of eggs in the holes. When the eggs hatch the nymphs crawl down or drop to the ground and burrow into the soil to live approximately 13 to 17 years and the cycle repeats. They do not bite and, after mating, die. There is no need to spray any chemicals as they are not considered a pest.

PANTRY PESTS

Always follow the Pesticide label, as it is the law.

Drug Store Beetles, Sawtooth Grain Beetles, Confused Flour Beetles, Rice Weevils, Granary Weevils, Indian Meal Moth, Angoumois Moth, Cigarette Beetles, Lesser Grain Beetles, Warehouse Beetles, Larder Beetles, and Khapra Beetles.

External feeder
Drugstore Beetle

External feeder
Sawtooth Grain Beetle 1/10 inch

External feeders
Confused Flour Beetle

Internal feeder
Rice Weevil

Internal Feeder
Granary Weevil

External Feeder
Indian Meal Moth

Internal feeder
Angoumois Moth

External Feeder
Cigarette Beetle

Scavenger feeder
Lesser Grain Beetle

External Feeder
Warehouse Beetle

External Feeder
Larder Beetle

Scavenger Feeder
Khapra Beetle

Mediterranean Flour Moth, Spider Beetles, and Almond Moths, Indian Meal Moth, Sawtooth Grain Beetle, and the Merchant Beetle.

Mediterranean Flour Moth

Spider Beetle

Almond Moth

Indian Meal Moth

Saw tooth grain beetle Merchant beetle

These pests and others are also known as stored food product pests. They all attack stored food products. These products include grain, dried fruits, seeds, nuts, biscuits, chocolate, dry dog food, bird seed, flour, cereals, beans, corn, dried noodles, and many other stored products. Infestations can occur in homes by bringing home food products from the store that are already infested. The can also be in stored food that has been opened in the past but not consumed yet. Dry pet food and bird seed can also be the source of an infestation, especially since these products are usually not in sealed containers. To eliminate these pests from a structure, you will need to find the products in which they are infesting and remove them, and treat the cabinets or areas they are located in. If you are dealing with a stored product pest that has a pheromone trap available, set them out to attract and kill the remaining adults. If you find them coming out from under the kitchen cabinets, you may have a mouse problem as well because mice will transport food and store it in a place that may not be accessible for you to remove. It may be necessary to remove the base cabinet kick plate and remove any stored food left by mice. You also may need to address a mouse problem. To help prevent re-infestation, make sure you explain to the customer that food products, spices, pet food or bird seed should be contained in tightly sealed containers and not stored for periods longer than 3 months. A helpful tip to you, if you need a longer period to save the food, putting the item in the freezer will also prevent a re-infestation from occurring.

PESTICIDE SAFETY!
Always Read the Label!

It is a violation of federal law to use any product in a manner that is inconsistent with its labeling. The label will tell you exactly what you need to know when using the product. After you have handled any pesticide you should clean your hands and face thoroughly with soap and water before eating, or drinking. When storing pesticides, you should store them in a secure location out of the reach of children, adults, or pets. When a pesticide container is empty you should triple rinse the container and destroy it so that it can no longer be used for anything else. You should not use a container for pesticides that was used for something else at any time.

Using Protective Equipment:

Before using any product, read the label! The label will tell you what protective clothing you should use. It is always recommended to wear long sleeve shirts, long pants and protective gloves when handling and or spraying pesticides. Be sure to use head and eye protection such as goggles and head gear such as a face hood whenever using a pesticide such as Demand CS outside to protect your skin around your face and eyes. Always make sure you use a filtering mask, respirator, or other standard protective clothing if you are spraying above your head. If you get this product around your temples next to your eyes it can cause a skin abrasion like a sunburn but will go away by the following day.

Use a respirator or an N-95 dust mask and throw-away gloves to avoid contamination in attics or crawlspaces.

RATS COMMENSAL

1. Identify the animal
2. Locate where it is
3. Determine the reason it is there
4. Develop a solution
5. Instigate the solution

Step 1. Identify a Rat Infestation.

A sign that a rodent could be in a home is an abundance of Bottle Flies flying inside the house. Most generally Bottle Flies are only around an area where something such as a dead carcass exists. Other signs would be to actually see the rodents, smell, or hear the rodents inside a wall such as gnawing sounds. You might find gnaw marks on items such as at door entries, gnawed through water supplies to dishwashers, or refrigerator ice makers. Rodents also at times might chew water hoses in your automobile. Other signs such as shredded debris behind seldom moved furniture, or workbenches. Rodents can cause frayed electrical wiring in the attic. Odors coming from heat registers in the floor, or even dogs and cats becoming excitable for no apparent reason can also be a clue to determining a rodent infestation. Most of the time, the rat will not be present, so you may need to identify the infestation by the feces left behind. Most rat feces will be dark brown to almost black in color. The feces will be from 3/8" to 3/4" long, and approximately 1/8" to 1/4" thick. You can determine the age of a dropping by its color. If it is dull in color, it's an old one. If it is shiny, it's a fresh one. You can identify a rat infestation by how stored items have been damaged with urine marks, or chew marks on them. Dusty hot water tanks or dry dusty crawlspaces with rodent footprints can also help you to identify a rat infestation. Tunneling in blown insulation of the attic looks like a snowplow came through. It is generally 4" to 6" deep and 3" to 4" wide. (Squirrel tracks are approximately 8" deep, and 6" wide.) Sometimes a change in water pressure can cause pipes to vibrate, or shake, and make you think you have a rodent problem. Check for signs of birds, raccoons, or squirrels that may have invaded your home. Check for bushes, trees, or even a loose cable wire against the house that might brush against the siding causing you to mistake the noise for a rat problem. Have you heard sounds, and if so, what time of day or night? Have you smelled any unusual smells, if so, where and when? Do the smells appear when the furnace turns on, or is it consistent all of the time? Have you had any natural gas fixtures installed or repaired recently? Natural gas can smell quite strong and there may be a leak that could be hazardous. Has any of your stored food in the pantry or other areas been disturbed? A few years ago, I got a call from an elderly lady who was having a tea party with two other ladies. It seems while they were visiting, one of them heard chewing sounds coming from the bedroom next to where they were having tea. I came out while the ladies were all still there. They took me to the room where the chewing sounds were coming from, and I too could hear it. I determined the sounds were coming from the top of the wall above the bed, so I took my shoes off and stood on the bed next to the wall. I thought if I pounded on the wall, the rat chewing would stop, so I gave it one good knock, and all three ladies were standing in the doorway watching me as I knocked. To my surprise, my hand went right through the wall. Unfortunately, it was a yellow jacket nest ready to break through. Even though I was standing on the bed, and all three ladies were in the doorway, I was the first one out of the room. So, be sure about a sound before you take action. Before you knock, check the outside area of the wall for bee activity outside at the same area.

Step 2. Locate the Rat Activity.

Inspect inside the house, garage, attic, crawlspace, storage shed, and the exterior of the house. You should always wear gloves and a good dust mask, or respirator when entering a crawlspace or attic to prevent air borne particles from contaminating you. Several diseases can be air borne such as, Murine Typhus, Bubonic, Jaundice, Histoplasmosis, and others.

Step 3. Determine the Cause of the Rat Infestation.

Sometimes you may forget to replace the batteries in your smoke alarms and when the batteries are worn down far enough, they begin to make a chirping sound that could make you think it's a rat caught in a wall, or ceiling. Do you own a pet? I find that the majority of my customers that have a rat infestation also have a pet. Where do you feed the pet? Where do you store the pet food? Do you have a cat or doggy door? Do you store bird feed? Do you store food in the garage or on the back porch such as onions, potatoes, or other garden vegetables? Do you feed the birds, or squirrels? Do you feed the neighborhood cat? Do you have any fruit trees, or vegetable gardens? Where do you put their garbage cans or bags? Do you leave any windows open, or overhead garage doors, or garage service doors open during the day or night? Many people leave their garage overhead door up 4" to 6" for ventilation or for their pet cat to come and go as it pleases. Do you do any composting outside? Do you police up any pet feces in the yard or in the garage? Have you done any remodeling in the last year? Sometimes remodeling may not be complete, and rats are getting in that way. When did you first start hearing or seeing evidence of rodents? Check for nesting areas outside such as tall grass, rubbish, low decks, dense bushes, rockeries, ground covering type plants, ground burrowing from rats, trees overhanging the house, or wood piles that are just loosely piled on the ground. Sometimes you might save things that you never need, or will use, but don't throw anything away, both inside the house as well as outside. To really get control of the problem, you need to understand the problem will persist until the clutter is removed. The rodents love to live in a place that they can hide in during the day.

Step 4. Develop a Solution.

Sometimes you may smell a strong odor in the house. If you determine it is from a dead rodent, this should be your first priority. If the rodent can be found, it should be removed and the surrounding area should be disinfected by means of a chemical neutralizer such as DSV sanitizer or Bac-A-ZAP (odor neutralizer.) If the rodent is in a place where it cannot be located or removed, such as in a wall or between the ceiling and a second floor above the room, you can attempt to eliminate the odor by injection of a neutralizer in the cavity, or use an ozone machine. An ozone machine sends out a negative charge in a molecular size that attaches itself to the odor molecule that has a positive charge. It then becomes heavier than air and falls to the floor, or ground, and out of the air patterns that we can smell. All the entryways must be corrected to stop the ingress of rats that are outside. Always place your traps just inside the point of entry to the crawlspace, or attic. The rats will find them, and it will be easy to retrieve the rats and the traps when the project is over. When controlling rats, you should never use poison bait in an attic, or crawlspace, as the rats can and will eat the poison bait if it is the only thing available. The problem is however, if they eat poison bait, they may die where you may not be able to retrieve the carcass. This can not only create a very bad smell, but can be a source for flies to breed in, and during the bloating period after death, the fluids from the rat can bleed through a ceiling or wall and cause a stain.

Step 5. Initiate the Solution.

Make a thorough inspection noting all accesses that need closing. Make a report showing where the accesses are and how to seal them off. Set up traps inside the house, and garage if they are found there, and in the attic, and or crawlspace. Make the existing repairs, or get a reliable contractor that can do the repairs. Unless the repairs are done, you can expect a continued problem inside until they are completed. After the repairs are done, you should do follow up trapping which will generally be completed within 7 days of the repairs being completed. The tooth enamel of a rat on the U.S. index hardness scale is 5.5; steel is above 6.0; iron is 4.0; aluminum is 2.0; lead is 1.5; and plastic is even less, and foam is even less than plastic, so sealing with anything less than the hardness of the tooth enamel of the rat will not stop them and will not fix the problem. A rat's jaw pressure is 24,000 pounds per square inch. Rats can chew through just about anything except steel. Rat populations rise in the summer because of less need for shelter and more abundance of food. In the winter, rats look for shelter, and the weak ones die because of the lack of food and shelter for the entire population. The fact that they are all interested in getting out of the cold is why you see or hear most of the rat signs in the winter months, but the reality of it is, the populations are less at that time. The rats came from outside, and are quite prolific. It would be impossible to totally eliminate their populations outside, but they can be reduced to a tolerable level by placing outside poison stations around the house. These stations should be serviced on a regular basis after all accesses to the structure are closed. After the repairs are completed, and the rats are trapped out, the motivation drops dramatically to install bait stations. If you were on a ship in rough waters, and suddenly you fell overboard, and one of the crew people said we've got a special on life preservers, would you agree to buy one at that time? What if the same ship was not in rough waters, but was in dry-dock and you were safely on the dock, would you still buy one? This is the same way you can feel when the rats are not running around in your house. After the repairs, check the traps and collect up the dead rats, and do an additional follow up to check and pull the traps if necessary, then set up outside poison stations. They should be serviced on a monthly basis for the best results. If you are not sure that all the rats have been removed by the traps, then set a paper plate in all the areas you had set traps. Place 10 peanuts on each plate and check the plates the following week. If none of the peanuts have been disturbed, you have got all the rats that were there inside. If you do not do the maintenance outside, you should know that rats mark their entry points into a building by urinating on them, and it's only a matter of time for the new rats that follow the scent of the old rats to find the old entries, and chew a new hole into the house again. Generally rats require 5 to 6 days to warm up to a bait station, and then mark the station with urine. A dirty station works best so I would only clean the station of debris when servicing it. After the first maintenance, determine if the rats are eating the bait. If they are not, then keep the stations there for at least 2 months to be sure.

RATS COMMENSAL RAT SENSES AND ABILITIES

A rat's gestation period is approximately 30 days, and females become sexually mature in 60 to 90 days. When her offspring become mature and reproduce, there can be as many as 7,500 rats from the original two rats in one year. This of course is based on optimum conditions, such as having enough food, water, shelter, and very little disease in the entire group. In the laboratory rats can live up to 5 years, however due to the stress on the population with a lack of shelter, food, water, and the presence of disease, the average life expectancy for a commensal rat is only about 6 months in the wild. Rats have fine sensory guard hairs that grow from the tip of their nose to their tail that have sensory organs at the base of the hair. They can literally feel their way through an area with these hairs at a full run. Rats also have a special part of their brain that can memorize their muscle movement when they are traveling along a particular route, and in total darkness repeat that same movement when they are startled. Most generally rats prefer to stay along a border of some kind such as traveling along a wall or through a tunnel. On occasion they will go across a room or crawlspace under a house or in an attic space once they have become familiar with the surroundings. Rats have a keen sense of smell that is 50 times greater than that of a dog, and will mark their scent with urine along an area so the rat and others can follow the scent. Rats can climb just about any structure provided that there is some kind of roughness or edge on the surface for them to cling to. They can also enter a building by walking across a wire such as a telephone or cable, or power line. Rats have a keen sense of hearing, so if a rat is in the attic, or crawlspace under the house, most generally when you enter the space it will have already left the immediate area by the time you enter. One interesting fact about rats is that if you shine a light straight at them it is possible to mesmerize them so that as long as you keep the light in their eyes you can walk right up to them and whack them. Rats can taste one part per million, so it is very important that baits do not get stored along with any cleaning supplies, or insecticides as the bait might be refused by the rodent. Dumpsters that have plastic lids can be replaced with the kind that have side metal doors instead. Policing up storage areas and raising shipping pallets up off the ground with planking and cement blocks at least three feet away from the building will reduce the hiding places rats can use. Providing a four-foot clear path around the entire exterior of the building will also help to reduce nesting sites. Setting up outside bait stations around the perimeter, and servicing them either each week, or at least every other week will go a long way to controlling rats. If you are concerned about how the bait stations will affect the landscaping, I recommend the "Rodent Rock" bait station as it looks and feels just like a landscape rock, and it is moderately priced so in most situations you can take advantage of its costs and looks.

Commercial Rat Problems

Most commercial rat problems have an element of non-compliance by one or more of the occupants on a commercial site, or it is simply not possible to eliminate all access points due to either construction design, or the way commercial doors are used. An example of this would be a loading dock door in many instances is left up during company operation hours, which can extend into the night. Another example is that restaurant kitchens generally leave the back door open for ventilation or deliveries. Strip malls can be a problem because the access could be on one end of the building yet the rats seem to be active only at the other end of the building and sometimes the problem is with tenants that won't accept the idea that a rat problem even exists.

Rats Commensal in Commercial Buildings

Always follow the Pesticide label, as it is the law.
Dumpsters can present a problem when tenants fail to keep the lid closed or the food garbage is just loosely thrown into the dumpster. Food producing plants and food storage buildings can provide a perfect environment for rat populations. As much as possible, all openings should be closed. Due to the design in most commercial settings the use of rodenticides is almost a necessity. Many things can be changed to reduce the rat populations around commercial settings, such as installation of heavy-duty screen doors with low profile metal thresholds on rear entries to restaurant kitchens. Tracking tubes can be installed around the perimeter near entry points, and dumpster sites. If a tracking tube is installed on the ground next to the building, rockery or landscaped area, I recommend that it be secured by a T stake on each end. If a tracking tube is installed on the ground next to the building, rockery or landscaped area, I recommend that it be secured by a **Permatite stake** on each end. Kness Snappy rat traps work better than glue boards in closets because of the possibility of items getting stuck in glue boards other than rats.

Rats in a Cathedral Ceiling

Sometimes rodents will get into a cathedral ceiling such as one that has rafters with 6" spaces between the ceiling and the roof, or even an attic space that is too low to access and doesn't actually have an access door. The rodent most likely entered via a roof joint, or through a broken bird vent on the end of the rafters. In this case the corrective measure is to cut a 10" x 10" square hole into the ceiling, and install a Kness Snappy rat trap with a 4' to 6' string attached to it, and a small stick attached to the end of the string. Temporarily close off the hole leaving the string hanging outside of it, then close the access points from outside, and within 4 to 5 days you will have caught the rodent. Pull the string attached to the trap and remove the rodent and then replace the square cutout and seal the joints.

Rat and Mouse accesses

Residential Mouse Control

Always follow the Pesticide label, as it is the law.

All of the same procedures for rat control also apply to mouse control. Exclusion should be done in the same way. Placing poison bait in the attic, or crawlspace under the house is okay for mice. Mice weigh approximately 1/4 to 1/2 ounce so if some die in an attic, or wall or crawlspace, the likelihood of an odor is not as great as a rat odor could be because a rat can weigh as much as one pound. Likewise the bloating of the body is far less apt to leak through a wall or ceiling and cause a stain from a dead mouse. An exception to this would be if there were a plenum return type of furnace. A plenum return system is a closed crawlspace system with a concrete floor throughout. The space acts as a cold air return for the furnace. In this kind of a system you would not want to place poison stations in it, as it would draw the odor through the furnace and blow the odor out all the registers. The most important devices inside the house would be paper glue boards and multiple catch boxes. Mice like to hang around in the furnace and utility rooms, but generally this is a dusty area too, so multiple glue boards work the best there. I would not place poison in the kitchen because it can either be exposed to pets and small children, or if a large number of mice are killed directly under the kitchen cabinets, an odor could be detected. Because mice have a very limited range in a house it is quite possible that the mice are not throughout, so closing off interior openings separating the mice from one room to another is very prudent. Bird seed is the best choice for a food bait for mice. Mixing bird seed with peanut butter, or cooking oil, and using it on paper glue boards, snap traps, or multiple catch boxes works very well. It is important that you block the areas off from children and pets. I don't recommend pellet sized poison for mice, as the majority of it will be stored instead of eaten and eventually can lead to an infestation of pantry type beetles. Most of the problems come when the mice store the bait under the kitchen base cabinets. A block poison keeps storing the bait at a minimum. Even though mice can find a way into the building regardless of how much exclusion work you do, if you are going to use poison baits, you want to be sure that no rats can get in and create a problem with odor, flies, and bloating stains. Mice are more prone to get into cupboards and on top of counters, so sanitizing those areas on a regular basis until all activity has ceased is a very good idea.

RAT

Satellite guard

Install wall guards around the satellite base so that rats are unable to access the base to climb up the pipe to get on roof.

L Screen

Pillar and post homes, and mobile homes can be accessed by rats from burrowing under the skirting and accessing the underside of the home. To prevent this from happening, dig a trench around the perimeter approximately 10 to 12 inches deep and 10 to 12 inches wide. Install 1/4-inch steel screen starting from the last 4 inches on the siding and attach the top of the screen to the building with screws (Pan head self tapping). Run the screen down to the bottom of the trench and out 10 to 12 inches away from the building and cover the screen with dirt. Install a 3-inch trim board at the top of the screen for aesthetic purposes. After the L screen is in place, set snap traps under the building with dried apricot bait. Check the traps in a few days and remove any dead rats.

L Screen

Cantilever structure (overhanging the foundation)

Cantilevers can be accessed by rats from burrowing under the skirting and accessing the underside of the home. To prevent this from happening, dig a trench around the perimeter of the cantilever approximately 10 to 12 inches deep and 10 to 12 inches wide. Install 1/4-inch galvanized steel screen starting from the last 4 inches on the siding and attach the top of the screen to the building with screws (flat head self tapping). Run the screen down to the bottom of the trench and out 10 to 12 inches away from the building and cover the screen with dirt. Install a 3-inch trim board at the top of the screen for aesthetic purposes.

Garage door bottom

Most overhead garage doors have a slight to medium swale at both ends of the doors in the concrete to allow rainwater to run away from the door rather than run into the garage. Sometimes the swale is too much, and leaves a gap that rats and mice are able to access the inside of the garage. To fix this problem you need to install an aluminum L bottom that you can fill the gap by attaching the aluminum angle L to the bottom of the door with nuts and bolts. Be sure to use a wood 2x4 to hold the bottom down closing the gap when you bolt the L to the roll up door. Most metal shops, suppliers can get this for you. Leave a 1/4-inch gap on both ends to allow the door to roll up and down freely. (Note: the bottom of the L should be under the door.) The L should be 3” tall and 2” wide.

Overhanging tree limbs

Trees should be trimmed back from the roof line two feet to prevent rats from accessing the roof and attic.

Ivy is an easy way to gain access to the roof and attic

Cut back ivy to below the soffit area.

Tree bands are installed to prevent rats from gaining access to the roof via a tree limb.

Using a roll of clear vinyl 1/16 of an inch thick that is 12 inches wide, cut a piece that will go around the tree and overlap the length approximately 6 to 8 inches past the end. Install at the top and bottom of the cut piece a plastic clip. Put the long side of the clip next to the bark behind the vinyl and the short portion on the outside of the vinyl. Install a dab of silicone caulking on

the inside of the short piece to make contact with the inside of the exterior vinyl. The clips should be put on the side of the tree that faces away from view from the people.

Install a tree band on tree

Install a tree band with growth clips, but before doing so, be sure to trim the excess off at the base of the individual fronds, or cut limbs that overhang the roof line, and cut the frond on the areas that the band will be placed to prevent bumps in the vinyl.

Overhanging tree limbs

This tree needs to be trimmed to be a minimum of 2 feet away from the roof line.

This is the same tree after trimming.

Either use a tree band or remove the tree.

Here's a challenge!

Dryer exhaust vent needs a basket cover to prevent rats or mice from entering the dryer exhaust pipe from outside.

Dryer Vent basket

Installed dryer vent basket to prevent rats and mice access to dryer hose that leads to the interior of the house.

Install a metal frame made from a metal drip cap to attach the basket. Use hex screws and inserts to secure the frame. Drill a hole at the top of the frame and install an eye screw insert to hold the basket secure.

Rain Gutter Downspout Wrap

Install a downspout wrap made from Plexiglas to prevent rats from climbing to the roof line. Screen base of downspout with 3/4" galvanized screen and screws to prevent rats from going up the inside spout.

BBQ Wall guards

The movable round lid of the grill should have an angle metal installed along the back side with slotted holes in the metal guard to allow the guard to move up and down on the screws to prevent rodents from entering the grill from behind. Using pan head screws with inserts, install Plexiglas under BBQ cleanout trays to stop rats and mice from entering the tray areas. Check for any vent openings to the housing of the BBQ as well.

Wood piles should always be elevated off the ground a minimum of 8 inches. Four eight-inch pier blocks should be set up to form an oblong square, and place planking on top, and then stack the firewood on top of the planking. Having an eight-inch space under the stacked wood will prevent rats from living under the pile of firewood.

RAT BURROWS

Always follow the Pesticide label, as it is the law.

Rat burrows can be dusted with Rozol Blue tracking powder, then pour pea gravel into the hole on top of the Rozol Blue tracking powder. Caution, Rozol Tracking powder is a restricted rodenticide and you need to have a licensed pest control person to administer the powder. See Pesticide label.

RATS
Trapping

Using cage traps can be more politically correct to catch a rat inside of the house or office building when people are there.

Euthanizing caged rodents

The best method to euthanize them is with carbon dioxide. First you would build a wooden box larger than the cage, you might want to build a box that will contain several cages to dispatch the rodents quicker. The wooden box should have a removable lid. It does not need to be airtight. After the box is built, install a hole at the lower side of the box. Install a hose fitting that a gas hose can adapt to. Obtain a cylinder of carbon dioxide from a welding supply, along with a gauge to administer the gas. Carbon dioxide is neither flammable, nor is it a poison. What it does is to displace oxygen. It is heavier than air, so when you turn the gas on, it fills the box with carbon dioxide, and pushes the air out of the top. The rodent dies from lack of oxygen. It is quick, cheap, quiet, and clean.

Fence ledge trap

The ledge trap is designed to catch rats running along a fence or wall ledge. Do not use bait on this, as they will smell it and stop to check it out. Rats always follow the same odor trail left by other rats. You can catch rats in the same area over and over. The rear shield protects the neighbors from getting caught with their fingers in the traps. This ledge trap can be screwed into the face of the wall with inserts, and removed when the rats have all been caught. Be sure to secure the traps to the wood base of the station with screws, and the wood base to the metal with adhesive.

Trapping with snap traps

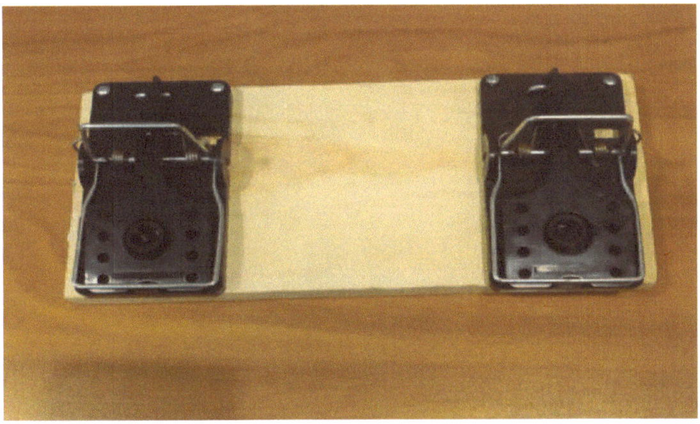

The best container to put a single trap inside that will prevent children or pets from accessing the trap I have found is the Bell Labs Protecta. Its square shape and inside space accommodates one Kness Snappy Rat trap very well. You can tell when a rat is caught because the tail will be sticking out of the entry about 3 inches when it is caught. I would suggest that these stations be baited with a small piece of dried apricot and the traps secured on the inside bottom by either Hercules putty, or glue, and setting a weight on top of the station to prevent it from being moved by children or pets. You should try to place the box next to a wall or under furniture next to the wall. It is generally most preferable that you secure it so if the box is accidentally bumped, it will not cause the trap to fire off. This rat trap is probably not the cheapest trap out there, but is the most reliable trap. Its unique design enables the user to easily set it, and when the rodent is caught it is not necessary to touch the killing bar to release the animal, as it has a secondary handle that allows the user to simply pull the bar back and the rodent is released. Most of the time the rodent never actually gets the bait, so re-baiting the trap generally is not needed. When trapping in an attic, or in a crawlspace under the house, or in a seldom used room, it is best to use two traps on a plywood board as seen above. This board will prevent a trap from being dragged to an area that is unreachable or inaccessible. The trap board can be just inside of the access area so it can be retrieved easily. The rat has a keen sense of smell and will find it.

Vertical Fence Wall Guard

Rats are able to climb up cinder block walls and wood fences and run along the wall and access the yard, and when they do, install a **Vertical Fence Wall Guard** that will keep them out for good. The guard should be 8 inches tall and have an L shape at the bottom of 4 inches wide, and run it the length of the fence. It should be made from 20-gauge galvanized steel. Overlap the ends by 2 inches. Drill into the top of the fence wall and insert screws and washers to secure the guard. Paint the guard the color of the wall as much as possible.

Vertical Fence Wall Guard

Vertical Fence Wall Guard

Vertical Fence Wall Guard

Horizontal Wire Guard

When telephone or power lines come down to the roof of your house, install this horizontal wire guard and this round stop to prevent the wire guard from sliding down the wire to the house. When the rat comes down the wire, this guard will tip over, throwing the rat to the ground. It automatically flips back into position for the next rat. The base of the guard has weights to keep the guard level until the rat gets on it.

Heat Box to form Plexiglas

Heat strip box for heating up sheet Plexiglas and forming the Plexiglas in various shapes.

Tracking tubes for rodents

Always follow the Pesticide label, as it is the law.

Tracking tube

Tracking tubes are most effective around dumpster areas, and commercial buildings. Use tracking tubes with tracking powder such as Rozol Blue inside of the tube. Start with a one by eight inch wood 6' long. Cut 6" PVC pipe in half lengthwise 5' long. Drill 1/2 inch hole in center of tube for installing dust with a bulb duster into the half tube. Place a waterproof signal label on the top center of the tube. Secure tube to the board with silicone cement, attach on both ends of the board with cement screws to a concrete surface. The tracking tubes are mostly used in dumpster areas. Dumpsters generally have food waste in them, and that is why the use of standard bait stations usually do not work well because the rats are already following the scent of food in the dumpster. The tracking tube is a tunnel that is attractive to the rodent and it will eagerly go in to check it out. The tracking powder inside of the tube will adhere to the feet of the rodent, and when the rodent cleans its paws before eating it ingests the toxicant and dies. Always install the tracking tube along some kind of a wall so the rat will be more apt to go through the tube. This product is a restricted pesticide and you should get a licensed pest control person to apply the dust for you.

RATS/FLIES

Sometimes you might discover a fly problem from having a rat die somewhere inside your home. You can obtain a fly machine to eliminate a fly problem from a dead rodent, or some decaying matter. This should only be used indoors. Be sure to check for a rodent or dead animal in the area, and make the necessary changes to eliminate the fly problem. Be sure to determine the kind of fly that exists so the proper method of correction is done.

Ozone machine eliminates odor

If you have a bad odor in the house, it can be from several sources. If it is a rat, and you cannot reach it via the ceiling or the wall, this ozone machine can remove the odors completely in approximately two weeks running 24/7. Be sure to read the instructions carefully, as adjusting the power too high can be over whelming and hazardous to the occupants by an excessive exposure.

Roof edge rodent guard

Install a flat sheet metal 10” by the length of the flat roof with 20-gauge galvanized steel to prevent rats from going over the roof from the ground. Secure the metal with screws and inserts. Paint the underside that is exposed to match the color of the building.

Rat accesses Wall guard

Prevents rats from accessing the roof.

Use a level and screws with inserts to secure the guard to the wall. Paint the guard the same color as the house.

This wall guard should be made of 22-gauge galvanized steel 20 inches long and 5 inches wide with a 45-degree angle bent on 1 inch. Drill 3 holes 1/8” inch evenly space on the 1-inch bend. Secure the guard to the area you want to stop rats from getting past it. Install wall inserts and screws through the 1-inch bend and attach it to the wall. Paint the wall guard the same color as your wall exterior. This guard will allow the rats to come down from

the roof, but will not allow them to come back up to the roof. I suggest that you have a local sheet metal company make the part for you.

Chimney Wrap

Rats can access the chimney flue to gain access to the interior of the house and access the roof and attic via climbing the rough surface of the chimney. To prevent the rat from accessing the roof, install a continuous wall guard around the chimney. (Picture below.) I recommend that the corners are mitered at a 45-degree angle for aesthetics.

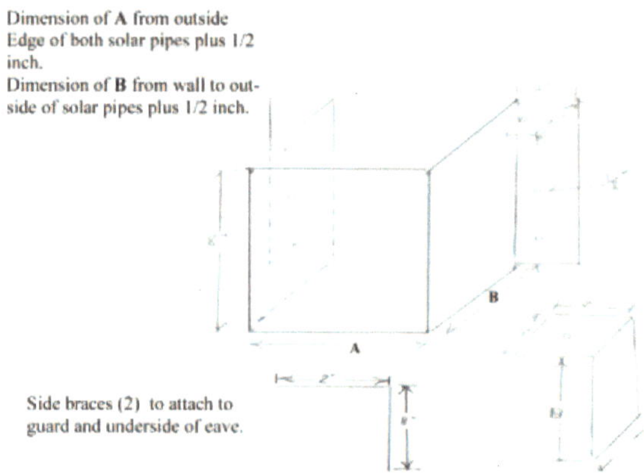

Solar pipe guard

Dimension of **A** from outside
Edge of both solar pipes plus 1/2 inch.
Dimension of **B** from wall to outside of solar pipes plus 1/2 inch.
Side braces (2) to attach to guard and underside of eave.

T Stake

This stake can secure any rodent station or tracking tube directly to the ground. This stake is made from steel rebar that can be welded by a welder. The handle is 5 inches long and the stake itself is approximately 24 inches or less.

Permatite rodent station stake

This stake is used to secure a rodent station to the ground by drilling with a rotor hammer a 1" hole in the ground and then using an electric hand drill to drill a 3/4" hole in the inside bottom of the station, then with the top handle of the stake tight, gently tap the stake into the ground until the handle of the stake meets the ground. Remove the handle, then set the station over and slide the top through the station and screw the handle back on.

Brick face crawlspace vent

Crawlspace vents through brick facing should be screened from inside the crawlspace with 1/4" galvanized steel hardware cloth. Use a heavy-duty adhesive to attach the hardware cloth.

RAT CONTROL WITH TRAPS AND RODENT FEEDERS

Always follow the Pesticide label, as it is the law.

Sometimes rats are trap shy, and will not go near the traps, or if they do, they are able to get the bait without getting caught. When a trap is introduced for the first time, and you realize that you have already used this kind of trap but with no results, I suggest that you bait the trap, but do not activate it. Allow 3 to 4 nights of feeding on it, and then come back and set it. If you are using the Victor wood stream trap, and not placed in a protective box, then you might want to bait it in the unset position for 3 to 4 nights, and on the fifth night place a layer of Kleenex over the entire trap. The rat will smell the bait and then attempt to claw through the tissue paper only to find he is caught in a very painful dilemma. Glue trays and glue board traps can work very well in a protected environment. For the best results you should attach the trap on to a 1/2-inch-thick plywood board so the trap cannot be moved by the rat. The area should not be dusty, or have a lot of items that could get caught on the board, or tray. A popular place to set the trap board is behind a couch, or piece of furniture. Avoid placing them next to curtains, or where small children might have access to them. Don't put them anywhere that pets may be able to touch them as it will not bc pleasant for the pet to get its hair caught in it. If your pet does get into the glue, you can use cooking oil to remove the pet's fur from the glue. Always attempt to have the glue boards placed along a wall that the rats travel frequently. Be sure to secure the glue board to the surface of the plywood either with Hercules putty, duct tape, tacks, or even screws. If they are not secured, the rat will bounce around on them until they are able to wedge themselves against something to get free. I have found that putting food bait on them to attract rats will generally keep the rats off of them when they realize the sticky surface exists. You really want to have them in their path, and have the rat stumble over them in the dark. Rats can die almost anywhere in a building unless the openings have been closed, and traps have been set to have a controlled kill. Besides smelling bad, or causing stains from body fluids, or causing fly problems, they can also act as a reservoir for pantry pests such as carpet beetles, larder beetles, drug store beetles, and several other insect pests. Most peak rodent activity occurs approximately one hour after dusk, and one hour before dawn, however when there is stress on the population from food shortages, the rats will change their patterns, and become daytime feeders. Over the last ten years we are finding the rodent populations are increasing at such an alarming rate that in some areas rats are becoming diurnal (daytime feeders). A rat's front paws have four fingers, and on the hind feet they have five toes. Knowing this can help you determine traffic patterns, and be able to estimate their approximate numbers in dusty environments. There are several different formulas of rodenticides, and each one has its own particular purpose. Weather blocks are easily secured into bait stations that will prevent them from being exposed when the station is tampered with. They also resist moist conditions of the surrounding turf in which they are placed. Granules can be placed in undisturbed areas in stations that are set where they cannot be accessed, or turned over by unauthorized persons, children, pets, and non-target animals. Water baits can be placed where there is an abundance of competition food such as dumpster areas, or food plants, food storage facilities, and any area where water is scarce or unavailable to the rat. Tracking powders can be used in burrows, or tracking tubes along peripherals of buildings and next to Dumpster areas. No matter what kind of bait you use, it is always a requirement to first read and follow the label directions precisely.

Accesses

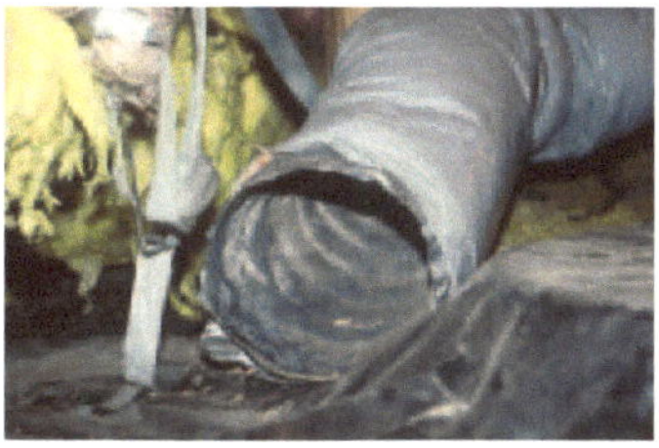

Crawlspace and attic cleaning and sanitizing and reconnecting broken heat ducts is an important thing to do as rats can carry several diseases that can be spread into the air ducts of your home. If your subfloor insulation is damaged, it should be replaced as well.

SAFETY EQUIPMENT

It is an O.S.H.A. requirement that when working on a structure that is over 4 feet in height, an individual must wear safety equipment such as a hard hat. In addition, I recommend that a body harness, and roof cleats be worn if the roof is of cedar construction, and has a pitch steeper than a 3/12, you should use a climbing rope that is securely anchored to prevent an accidental fall.

Use Safe ladders. Ladder with Leg Levelers

Safety hood

Always follow the Pesticide label, as it is the law.
It is important that if you spray above your head with pesticides, or during a windy day outside that you wear a hood and safety goggles to avoid getting the spray on your face or in your eyes. Some sprays such as Demand CS can cause a light sunburn around your temples. This is a temporary situation which generally clears up the following day. To avoid this possibility, you should always wear a safety head hood such as the one in the picture below. It can be hand made and sewed together. I recommend that you have it made out of soft material and in your skin like tone to avoid scaring small children that they think it doesn't match your own skin.

Safety rope and harness

Always follow the Pesticide label, as it is the law.

SCORPIONS

Always follow the Pesticide label, as it is the law.
Scorpions (Bark or sometimes called Sculptured) This animal is in the **arachnid family** (spiders). Their tail has a stinger that they use to subdue their prey and for defense. **Scorpions are very common in the southwest**. There are several species found in the southwest, but only one of them is considered a serious threat to man and his pets. It is called the bark scorpion, or sometimes referred to as the **Sculptured Scorpion**. The body is approximately 2" to 3" in length and is light brown in color. This scorpion has established itself in various locations of the southwest states. If they are in the attic they are attracted to lighting in the attic such as recessed ceiling lights, however the light fixture is too hot to pass through until the light is turned off. After the light has cooled, the scorpion enters through the small openings in the fixture. When they get into the home they walk along the ceiling and down the interior walls. They can be a very serious threat to you during the day and night when things are moved or disturbed where the scorpion may be hiding. Scorpions can invade a home when the doors or windows are left open, but may come in on moving boxes, or stored items in the garage and hide behind hanging pictures, and in closets. After dark they come down from the walls and other areas they can be hiding in, and become a serious problem for the occupants of the house. They climb trees outside and can be knocked off of a limb or foliage by simply a person or pet dog or cat brushing up against the foliage. If a person is stung by a bark scorpion, immediate medical attention is strongly advised. Small children, older adults, or someone with a weak immune system, and even the family pet may require hospitalization if they are stung. Control of scorpions would include the removal of debris such as piles of lumber, and old accumulation of junk items in the yard. The exterior perimeter wall of the house should be sprayed 3 feet up the wall, and the wall or fence that separates the property from your neighbors all around your home sprayed the same way with a water-based pesticide such as Lambda Cyhalothrin (Demand CS at .06%) mix; this is very suc-

cessful in killing scorpions. In addition, the attic should be fogged or sprayed with the same material. All door entry areas should be sprayed from the access door out to 4' from the door. To eliminate the scorpions from inside your house. An inspection of the access doors should be done making sure there are no cracks at the base of the doors that you can see light coming through. If light is coming through, then use a putty or rubber strip to seal off the light areas. Check the garage for expansion joints in the concrete floor. If the light appears from outside through at the V expansion joint while the garage is dark, use a ready to use cement mix to seal the joint with a 3" putty knife where the roll up door contacts the joint. Do not attempt to seal the side openings of the door at the guide rails. Perform spot broadcasting spray on the garage floor areas where possible. Inside the house, all pets, children and adults should be out of the treatment areas until all sprayed areas are completely dry. Birds should be removed for 24 hours and if a fish aquarium exists, be sure to cover the tank and turn off the air pump. Place the pump air receiver above the floor areas so as not to accidently spray it. All toys, shoes, magazines, pet dishes, and other loose items should be moved away from the walls of the rooms and closet floors. Spray along the base boards throughout the house approximately a 4" wide path every 3 feet. Scorpions are nocturnal and travel at night. They have very poor eyesight, so they tend to walk along the base boards. Always ask your family or guest or anyone that is in the house if they suffer from upper respiratory problems. If anyone does, they should be out for a minimum of 72 hours and have the house well ventilated before they come back in. It's a good idea to have them check with their doctor with the information of the products. MSDS form or the label of the product.

PSEUDO SCORPIONS

Always follow the Pesticide label, as it is the law.

The Pseudo scorpions are not harmful to people as they do not have a tail with a stinger. Their food prey are small insects. To subdue their prey, they grab them with their claws and there is a toxicant in their claws that kills the prey. These tiny arthropods are not scorpions at all, but belong to the spider family. They are approximately 1/8 inch in length. There are about 2,500 different species in the world. If you want them destroyed in the house, spray as a crack and crevice along baseboards and outside around the foundation with Demand CS at .06%.

I recommend outside monthly ongoing maintenance at .03%, The Pseudo scorpion's life span is up to 3 years.

SPIDERS

Always follow the Pesticide label, as it is the law.

With the modernization of travel and the improvement of roads throughout the United Sates, our country has become very mobile. Even though certain spiders are not indigenous to our area, they can be brought into your state by means of hitching a ride in moving vans, cars, motor homes, trains, buses, suitcases and any cargo that is shipped in freight. With this in mind we must look at the possibility that any venomous spider that is out there surely can be found anywhere in the USA. There are only about five species of spiders in the USA that that have been found thus far that are considered harmful to man. These are the Black Widow, Desert Brown, Recluse, Hobo spider, and the Yellow Sack spider. Black widow spiders can be found in every state in the U.S. but are more abundant in the southern states. Most adult Black Widow females are a shiny jet black in color and have two reddish triangular or hourglass design markings on the underneath of their abdomen. Their body is about 1/2 inch in length. Brown Recluse spiders are generally found in the Gulf States. They can be found in other areas; however, it would be because they were transported in from their natural habitat via commercial and or household movement. Desert Brown recluse adults are usually tan to dark brown with a darker fiddle-shaped marking on the top of their body. The length of their body is about 1/4 to 1/2 inch. There are a number of different species of Black

Widows and Brown Recluse spiders, which can differ a little from the descriptions above. The Hobo or Aggressive House spider is approximately 3/8 to 5/8 inch long, and has a chevron marking on the top of the abdomen. They look very similar to the Brown Recluse spider in size and color but do not have the dark brown fiddle-shape on them. Not only do they look similar, but their bite reacts similarly too. The Yellow Sack spider is approximately 3/8 of an inch length of their body. Spiders reproduce by building a silken sack and lay small eggs in it, and depending on the specie of the spider will hatch out in various amounts from 250 to 500 new spiderlings. When the spiderlings come out of the sack they climb up as high as they can on a house or tree limb and weave a one strand web and wait for the wind to pick up and then release the web and float on the wind to a new location where they can catch insects without the competition of the other spiders. Spiders often enter buildings through small cracks and crevices on the structure or from firewood or other items being brought into the house. A thorough inspection of the inside and outside is recommended to determine the numbers and areas to spray. Demand CS at .06% is the best product to use spraying along baseboards inside and around windows, and door frames outside and the outside foundation areas, as well as eaves of the house.

Black Widow spider

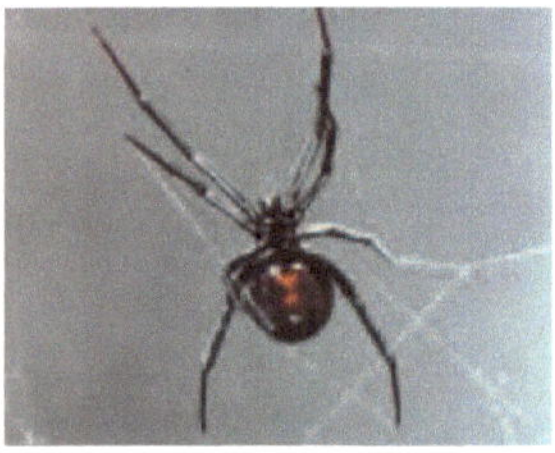

Hobo Spider

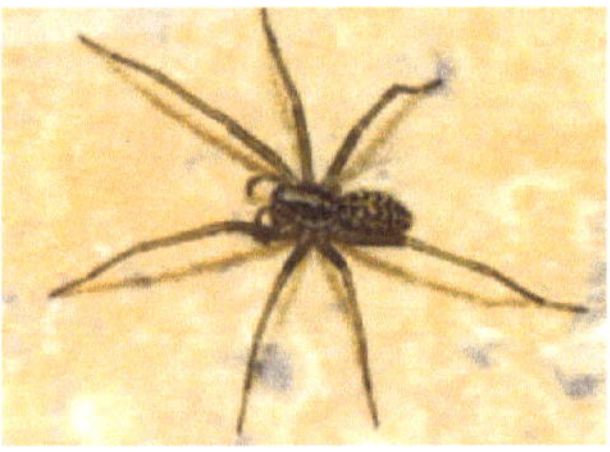

Desert Brown recluse

Yellow Sac Spider

Sun Spider, Wind Scorpion, and Camel spider are all the same arachnid

They are not Scorpions; they belong to the Spider family. These spiders for the most part live in burrows in the ground. They feed on other insects and arachnids. They have very large jaws and are capable of attacking rats, mice, lizards, small snakes, and outside cockroaches. They do not have a venom, however they can cause a very bad bite that will need to be cleaned and seen by a medical service to avoid an infection. The chemical of choice is Demand CS at a maximum of .06% rate spraying the area they are found in.

Tarantula

Always follow the Pesticide label, as it is the law.

Tarantulas are found in areas near the desert. Most of the ones found are burrowers. They can bite but do not cause fatality to humans or pets such as dogs and cats, however the bite can be very painful for several days. The female can live up to 30 years, however the males generally live about 7 years. There is no need for pest control unless you want to control the numbers. If a maintenance is needed simply spray an outside normal spray (see the label) with Demand CS at .06% on a monthly basis.

STORY BY LYLE

A long time ago when life was much simpler than it is today, lived a young girl of eighteen, named Pamela. She lived in a small cottage just off the edge of the wooded forest, on a belt known as Tickerton Glade, just north of Scotland. The year was 1371 AD. Pamela was the older sister of three other children, Thomas who was twelve years of age, Benson nine years old and Silvia who had just turned six years last March. Their parents James and Lila both worked very hard for the King of Scotland as a wood chopper and a hand maiden. Times were very hard for the family. The winters were cold and brutal, and the summers were hot and unbearably humid. Like all subjects of the royal family, it was required that James and Lila work at the castle from sunup to sundown all week long, except for Sunday. On Sunday there was rest and family communion. During this period of time, King Leavenhoff and her majesty Queen Arla were dedicated to the church and for the most part ruled with a just and gentle manner. Life in general was very difficult. There were no modern conveniences like running water, indoor plumbing, electricity, modern medicine or any other items we take for granted. The average life expectancy even for nobles was twenty-seven years old. What little food that could be harvested in bleak years could not be preserved long enough to make it through the cold winters, but still for the most part people were generally happy with what they had. Pamela was a kind and mild-mannered girl who often would daydream about how life would be if she could only meet a nice boy and fall in love. Her passion for life was strong, even while she labored for hours each day to keep the children clean and the house chores done. Their house was only twelve feet by sixteen feet in size but had a dug-out cellar area where they kept what little food they managed to grow stored. Whenever the rains came, the cellar would flood and everyone had to scramble to get the food to a higher location. They lived by a small stream that Thomas the oldest boy would fish and get fresh water for the family from. Benson the younger brother spent most of this time hunting in the forest. Sometimes he would come back with a fox or raccoon, but many times the best he could get would be a couple of muskrats or other small animals. Silvia the youngest girl was very quiet. She just played with her little rag doll that Pamela had sewn for her out of some old rags that were too raggedy to serve as parts for any clothing anymore. This period of time became the most important period of time in history and it all began with this meekly family. After returning from the castle where she delivered her mother and father's noon meal, Pamela stopped along the stream to watch the fish in a small pool area where the water was crystal clear and very deep. As she gazed into the pool, she noticed she was being watched by a young lad of nineteen. She was at first startled, but as the lad approached she could see he was smiling and gestured for her acceptance to allow him to come closer.

"My, what a beautiful day it is!" he exclaimed. "My name is Eric, might I ask you the favor of allowing me to join you?" She smiled and bid him welcome. "Where hence do you live?" She said in a timid voice. "I live just over the hill beyond the river's bend," he replied. "I've never seen you before," he said. "You are such a catch! Have you a lass that courts?" "No," she said quietly. "What be your name?" he inquired. "I was born as Pamela of Tickerton Glade. My family are servants of the royals. My father chops wood and my mother a hand maiden." "How is it that you are not married, might I ask? For you are near my age," he exclaimed. With an embarrassing reply she retorted, "I would ask you the same, but not in that fashion." Seeing his mistake, he bowed his head with apology. "My lady, I have offended you and with this I bid you well and take my leave." "No, do not go, it is I who have caused you stress. Please sit down and let's visit."

Pamela and Eric stayed by the pool for at least an hour, then Pamela said she had to get back to her home, as it was nearing the time her siblings would return and would want dinner. "May I see you again?" Eric inquired. "Yes," she replied and then they parted.

The next day Pamela was very excited to take the mid-day meal for her parents to the castle, as she was sure Eric might be near the pool. When she approached, to her delight he was waiting patiently near the same area. "How are you today, Miss Pamela of Tickerton Glade?" Eric said in a confident voice. "I am very happy and pleased to see you again, Sir Eric," as she cried with a giggle. "I have heard talk at the castle that Queen Arla has become ill and one of the knights has also befallen the same," exclaimed Eric. "Something about the wine that she drinks, it may be poisoned. They suspect the cellar keeper. If she gets worse, they are sure to blame him, and he will be executed." "Oh my, I would not want this fate," said Pamela. Just then a horseman riding very fast went right by them shouting, "The queen is dead, the queen is dead!" Eric jumped up and started to weep. Pamela didn't know what to think? "Why are you so upset?" Eric turned very pale and said in a voice very broken and soft, "The queen is my mother. I'm Prince Eric of Tickerton Glade..." Pamela was shocked and humbled to learn that Eric was of the royal family. She tried to comfort him as he wept from the news of his mother's death. "I must go to my father the king as he will have no one to comfort his grief." As Eric left Pamela standing there, she watched him with a silent sigh. She knew Eric was in great sorrow. Over the next two days people began to speculate what would become of the cellar keeper, as his fate of execution was surely sealed. Much to the surprise of everyone, the king did nothing. The royal funeral was announced throughout the kingdom. Great sadness seemed to linger for three more weeks as the rule began to emerge from its recluse manner. The king decreed that anyone who could discover the cause of the queen's death shall be granted anything they wished that the royal could muster. Many scholars and learned teachers began to investigate the cause. One such investigator who was a playwright and mentor to many decided to study the queen's habits. He felt that all things are physical, and by enough research he could determine the cause of death. This investigator went by the name of William Shakespeare. After looking at the wine in the cellar and serving it to several animals over and over, he decided the wine was not poisoned.

His first question was why the queen and the knight who died a few days later were affected by the very same wine that others of lower stature were not befallen. After observing the glasses and cups the wine was served in, he suddenly realized the cause was very simple, he said to the king, "The royal drank from a pewter lead cup, as the lowly servants drank from wood carved cups." The lead pewters were poisoning the royals. With this information the king had all the pewter melted down and decreed that all utensils be of silver or wood. Shakespeare was so welcomed by the royals to have all that he wished that he wished to only be able to produce his writings to plays. He was so granted and funded by the king. Two years passed and Pamela and Eric fell in love. The king was beside himself as Pamela was a servant without the benefit of royal blood. Eric, on the other hand, did not care and resounded to his father he would give up his stature to be with Pamela. In time, the king accepted his son's request and a royal wedding was announced. All the subjects of the kingdom were in attendance. It was a gala event that any other royal wedding could not match. Pamela now was a part of the royals and could provide a happy and rewarding life to her parents and siblings. All seemed so right for three years. One day, Pamela's father and youngest brother Benson both became very ill. They both had fevers and both began to get dark red spots around their necks and chests. The royal medical sorcerer tried to cure them with special brews and incantations, but they only got worse. In just a short few days, they developed white rings around the red spots that had begun to spread to other parts of their bodies and they also began to grow in numbers and darken to almost a blacken blotch. A peculiar bitter odor also started to come from their blotches. After a few more weeks, both Pamela's father and younger brother passed away. It was very sad around the family. As time continued, other people in the kingdom started to get sick with these same symptoms. First just a dozen or more people, and then after six months there must have been over 1,000 people infected with this strange disease.

Even William Shakespeare's son Hamlet had been befallen with this horrible disease. The king finally decided to go to the clergymen and seek God's help. The clergymen stated that this disease was a sign from God that the sins of the kingdom were the cause. It was decreed by the king anyone who did not attend church on a regular basis was deemed to be the cause of the disease, and shall be put to death. In his heart the king knew that his people were very devoted to the church and that there must be another reason. A few months had passed and the deaths continued. Shakespeare's own son died. Shakespeare was so painfully saddened that he wrote a play in memory of his son. It was called "Hamlet". People began to get this disease so quickly that many walked around in the streets aimlessly. The odor that emanated from them was quite pronounced that everyone began to carry flowers in their pockets to mask the odor. People were dying so fast that they gave up on burying them. They simply piled them up in the street and burned the bodies. After 200 years, the disease began to take its toll, as more than 10 million people died. A children's nursery rhyme was written about the disease. It went like this: Ring around the rosy, pocket full of posies, ashes, ashes, we all fall down. The cause of the disease was finally discovered to be a virus strain in fleas that were carried by rats. When the rat died from the disease, the fleas would jump off and take a new host such as people. The disease could also be spread by touching a person that had the virus. This disease still kills several hundred people each year throughout the world. Even in the United States fifteen to twenty people die from it each year. What is the disease? Bubonic plague, commonly called the black death.

CPSIA information can be obtained
at www.ICGtesting.com
Printed in the USA
LVHW072056080422
715715LV00001B/13
9781638673309